The Past Be But Prologue?

Executive Curriculum Vitae
of Salman A. Nensi

NENSI.COM

The Past Be But Prologue?

Executive Curriculum Vitae
of Salman A. Nensi

Zariqa
Est. 2021

Zariqa.com

NENSI.COM

Table of Contents

GLOBETROTTING, FOUNDATIONS, DEDICATIONS, AND CHARLIE

Welcome Message | Map of Where Sal's Worked, Travelled, and Consulted | Foundations: Beyond Reports and the Nensi Family Foundation | Dedications ... and Charlie

Welcome

"Should everything go horribly wrong and everything screw up, he's going to be able to patch together a solution nobody knew was possible. Lastly, no review of Sal's abilities would be complete without mentioning that he is always able to find the best food and the best restaurants in any city. It is a gift that those around him rely on for the perfect business meetings."

WILLIAM HOPPER
Author at ERIS

For over three decades I have coordinated all aspects of message delivery, from brand development to internal reporting, for clients around the world. As an innovative thinker, I find solutions to problems that others consider intractable. I have worked in over thirty countries with differing languages, cultures, and sensitivities, and my network extends across more than ninety countries. This range enables deep insight into each project I tackle. My holistic, thoughtful, and well-planned contributions lead to streamlined and effective communications.

My clients tell me that I am often able to find solutions where none were thought to exist and that I ensure a job gets done efficiently and properly. I am a good facilitator, with a specialization in getting the most out of creative individuals who may not always work effectively in the corporate world. I also have over twenty years' experience in publishing, writing, editing, production, design, distribution, and new technologies.

One of the things I love doing in my spare time is travelling. I have been fortunate enough to have clients and work that has allowed me the freedom to travel and this is a great joy. Another interest is food and cooking. In my travels I have had fabulous days of market shopping and cooking in the most amazingly bizarre kitchens in Bhutan, Nepal, Tibet, Bangladesh, Korea, and China.

Inside you will find additional information on my skills and experience. At nensi.com, you can view my LinkedIn profile, download the short version of my CV. You can also see some of my published works at Zariqa.com.

Thank you for your time.

Map of Where Sal's Worked, Travelled, and Consulted

"While many people are reasonable planners, very few have the energy and drive necessary to consistently put complex plans into motion and see each step executed flawlessly. Mr. Nensi's creative energy has been a huge asset to my company and I unhesitatingly give him my strongest endorsement."

ALEX KAMMER
Producer, Gamehole Con

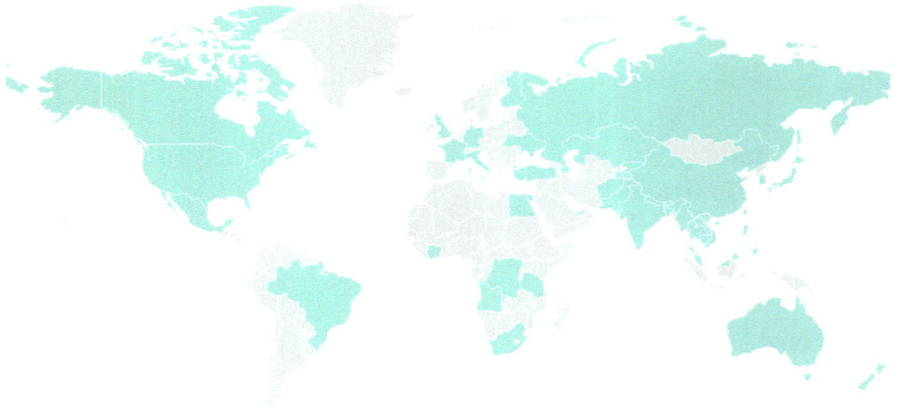

BEYOND REPORTS FOUNDATION

"I am really impressed by your courtesy. You are perhaps the nicest person on earth, who gives suggestions & ideas free of cost."

ASIM IFTIKHAR
Design Engineer at KSB Pumps Company Limited - Pakistan

Communications Consultant

Using 30+ years of experience in over 2 dozen countries Nensi answers any and all communications and marketing related questions for your NGO . . . pro bono.

From simple questions such as "My printer wants to know if my cover will be a bleed, what does he mean?" to more complicated scenarios such as, "We'd like to impart this health message to the rural population of this country; what is the best way to go about it?" to budget and timelines, "A supplier wants to charge us X dollars for Y job and says it will take Z weeks; is that a fair and honest price?"

Now with additional access to the DRPZ Communications group of consultants, Beyond Reports can offer advice and input on virtually any and all communications concepts, projects, vehicles, budgets, etc. . . .

If you are a legitimate NGO, please do be in touch. I would love to help. Please contact me via the Beyond Reports web site (https://beyondreports.co.uk/).

NENSI FAMILY FOUNDATION

"With great thanks for introducing us to the world of publicity with such comfort and style."

LAUREN COWEN
Author of *Daughters and Mothers* (Courage Books)

Early Childhood Education

In 2008 I was in Bangladesh. I made repeated calls on a tailor for some suits. There was an 8-year-old boy working there. Six days a week, 8-10 hours a day, earning his family a coveted 500 Taka a month. That's $6.44 USD. He opened the door for customers and would fetch tea, coffee, or cold drinks, and a variety of other small jobs. I asked the tailor if it would not be better if the boy (Abu) was in school?

The tailor replied that yes, it would be better-but Abu's family was too poor to do without the monthly income AND pay the required school fees. This was the beginning of the foundation.

Through the tailor I asked the boy's father if he might be interested in help from an outsider and the father agreed. Then I asked the boy if he would prefer to be in school instead of working—his answer was an enthusiastic 'Yes!'

With the help of some friends we arranged to have the boy's salary paid directly to the father and his school tuition directly to the school. A small budget was given to the family for school supplies and safe transportation to and from school. Having never been to school before, Abu was at the top of his grade within a year. By the end of the second year he was one of the top five students in the whole school.

This was how the foundation began. Dedicated to helping families in-need provide early childhood education for their children, The Nensi Foundation provides logistical and financial assistance. The Nensi Foundation for Early Childhood Education is a private institution and receives no government or additional funding from any other source. The foundation currently operates in Bangladesh and Cambodia.

Please use the contact form at Nensi.com if you would like to know more or, perhaps, help out?

DEDICATIONS . . . AND CHARLIE

In the beginning . . . there was Charlie.

Charlie was a gift given to me before I was born . . . and who, until a recent arm injury, used to travel with me everywhere in my hand luggage and was a good conversation piece at airport security. Traveling with parents while young Charlie had his own passport and a cape. He wore the cape for about 40 years until we got to Kathmandu. There we got Charlie a new wizard's outfit (pictured above) and I got a pair of jester slippers that matched those of my friend's kid's tiny jester slippers. Naturally I put mine in place of hers and sat at the top of the stairs to see what would happen in the morning. I was not disappointed but failed to get a good picture so you get Charlie.

After Charlie's inspirations came some actual people who fostered a sense of wonder and inspiration and love of science fiction, hope for the future, permission to dream and once I started, they were there to share the joys they wrought. As this CV project became more of a Catalogue of Me; it felt important to acknowledge these people, especially . . .

- Garfield & Judith Reeves-Stevens
- Terry & Judine Brooks
- Marlene & Bill José*
- Dave Duncan*
- Dennis Johnson*
- Pete Davison*
- Surat Toymastov*

*Are you resting in peace or enjoying the next adventure? Either way, you are sorely missed.

EXECUTIVE SKILLS & EDUCATION

OVERVIEW

Creative and organized management professional with experience in holistic ontology, capacity building, business development, strategic communications, project management (including publication, social media, and event management); consumer and trade marketing; sales and contract negotiations; new media technologies, writing and production.

Six Communication Specialties

1. Business Development/Project Catalyst
2. Communications Project Management & Services Contracting
3. Capacity Assessment
4. Capacity Building—Internal Messaging
5. Sales & Marketing—Outbound Messaging
6. Ontological Project Vision & Outcome Planning

Four Part Management Skill Set

1. Strategic/Management
2. Leadership
3. Creative Communication
4. Teaching, Training & Lecturing

EXECUTIVE SKILLS SUMMARY

"Sal is one of those rare project managers who actually has the skill to unite a culturally and geographically diverse team to focus on a single outcome, even when costs and deadlines are constrained. His international experience has been gained largely from working on-site in remote locations, giving him a unique understanding of global issues and the various requirements they produce."

JON SOUTHURST
Co-Founder at Talon Media Group

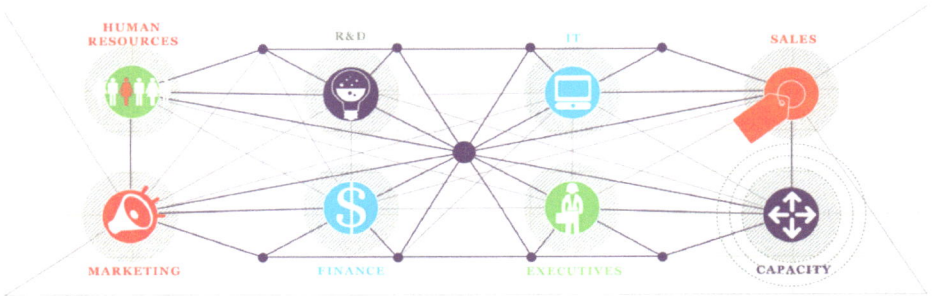

After receiving a BA in Mass Communication from York University in Toronto, Canada, Nensi then moved to research as well as becoming a published author. This led to lecture series across Canada, Beijing, Seoul, and Central Asia on the topics of media relations, technology, publishing, marketing, and business presentations. As managing director of The Omikron Group Inc., a communications firm (established 1988), Nensi handled marketing, branding, and promotional strategies for publishers, firms, and creative clients. These efforts covered multiple communications platforms.

Working at Beyond Reports, Nensi coordinated publication projects and provided communications, marketing, website, and systems consulting for various corporations, NGOs, and United Nations agencies, with many of them in the developing world. Processes were coordinated at every step, including hiring the creative talent, working with technical staff, as well as distribution. The goal was to help clients realize their communication projects within their budget while fostering their untapped in-house talents. He could often find solutions where none were thought to exist, while ensuring the job was done properly and efficiently. Nensi was able to get the most out of creative individuals, due to his twenty-two years of experience in publishing, writing, editing, production, design, and distribution.

Nensi has provided capacity building globally in many areas of marketing and communications, specialising in media management training. In addition he provides capacity building in print and web design, photography, event design and planning, as well as in marketing and communications plan generation.

In addition, Salman Nensi has decades of experience selling and marketing products, from fast-moving consumer goods to arts and cultural products. He has worked for NGOs, arts organisations, governments, ministries, and others who are selling ideas and concepts rather than products and units. In addition, he is experienced in creating all types of marketing vehicles, from traditional print-based to broadcast to new technologies, as well as multiformat and multiplatform campaigns. Nensi is experienced in creating all types of marketing vehicles required for non-products. He can provide assistance with everything from small projects that need finishing to larger ideas that need to be conceived of from the ground up.

Nensi sees ontology not just as technical patches that allow old computer systems to talk to each other. Ontology and semantic integration must go hand in hand, and coordinate with enterprise application integration. Full integration of hardware, software, systems of organization, suppliers and both the creators and recipients of messages is what an organization needs, and Nensi is ready to assist.

EXPANDED SKILLS LIST

"Whatever the project you're working on, Sal has the unparalleled ability to see the big picture, cut through the extraneous garbage, and help you look like a winner. He's intolerant of mediocrity and is definitely someone you want to work with if your goal is excellence."

MARK RUSSELL
Editor, writer, and other word stuff

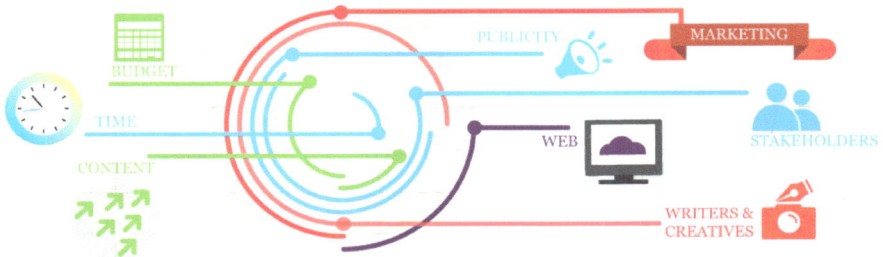

Strategic/Management Skills

Holistic Ontology
Business Development
Strategic Communications
Project Management
Media Relations/Publicity
Social Media Management
Crisis Control Communications Planning

Leadership Skills

Project Catalyst, Facilitation, Management
Corporate Communications Skills
Communication Services Contracting
Organizational Communications and Public Relations
Government Relations

Creative Communication Skills

Localization/Globalization
Publishing (including book design) & Agenting
Content-based Marketing & Communications (Tri3 Planning)
IP Management
Worldbuilding
Writing, Editing, Producing
Event Management

Teaching, Training & Lecturing Skills

NGO oriented communications training;
for more please visit BeyondReports.co.uk

Capacity Building, Organizational Structure and
Behaviour Consulting within Organizations

Redefining personal and office places and spaces;
for more please visit RedefineYourSpaces.com

Job Search and Career Growth Strategies
Media Relations Lecturing
Holistic Integration: horizontal, vertical, and circular lectures
Publicity Strategy and Materials Facilitations
Publishing—philosophy and practice in the 21st Century lectures

EDUCATION

Entrepreneurship in Emerging Economies
HarvardX, online course audit
Fall, 2021

- An interdisciplinary approach to understanding and solving complex social problems and how to address these problems across emerging markets.
- Taught by: Tarun Khanna, Jorge Paulo Lemann Professor, Harvard Business School, Harvard University.

Bachelor of Arts
York University, Toronto/Canada
09/87–05/91

- Honours interdisciplinary double major in Mass Communication (economics of) and Political Science (International Relations focus).
- News Reporter, Political Analyst, Columnist, and Arts Writer for: Excalibur, Canada's largest student-run newspaper (circulation: 22,000 bi-weekly).

• Founding Chair: Mass Communication Student Federation.
• Secretary: York Federation of Student's Club's Coalition.

Secondary School Graduation Diploma and Honours Diploma
Thornlea Secondary School, Markham/Canada
09/82~06/87

• Founded a school newspaper, The Hall Street Journal, and managed it for 3 years.
• Ran or participated in over a dozen after school activities for many years, such as

  ◦ student council
  ◦ yearbook sections editor
  ◦ commencement committee
  ◦ awards night committee

PREVIOUS POSITIONS

"Salman is one the most incredibly articulate, well-read, well-rounded and capable marketing professionals I have met in the last few years. His ability to manage, see and respect the most minute of details while consistently observing and pursuing strategic imperatives gives Salman the ability to be a superior leader and excellent mentor. His perennial good nature, strong sense of humour and ability to relate to virtually anyone makes having him a part of the team a true pleasure."

BOURKE MARRISON
Bell

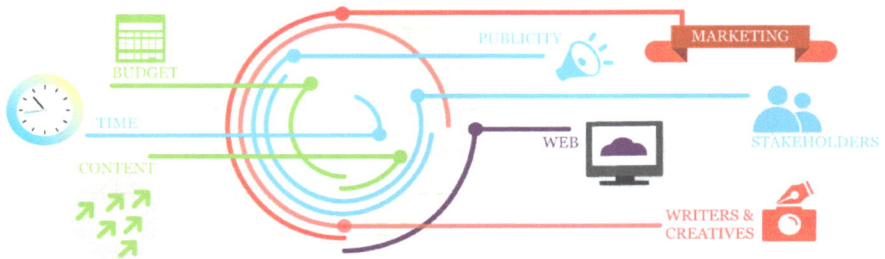

- **DRPZ Communications, Business Development & Project Director**
  - Africa-based consulting projects
    - ► Property Manager, Angola Developments
    - ► Redefine Your Places and Spaces project for Cruzerio, Luanda
    - ► Sales territory roll out and marketing plan for Safi Juice
    - ► Business development planning for
      - ▲ Aremh Manufacturing and
      - ▲ Azzero Company (South Africa)
    - ► Angolan Urban Gardening Project (Luanda, Soyo, and Cabinda)
  - Publisher, DRPZ Publishing
    - ► Fall of Ancients
    - ► The Kitchen Sink Magazine
    - ► Fire Hornet Codex
    - ► Tiny Hands Press
    - ► Hobb's Editions
    - ► Peppershot Press
    - ► Muttonchop Editions

- Nensi.com, Business Development & Project Director
- EBR Holdings Pte, Ltd (Singapore), Business Development & Project Director
  - Managing Director, The Ed Greenwood Group & Onder Media Group
- Beyond Reports, Business Development & Project Director
- The Omikron Group Inc., Managing Director, Principal Agent & Publisher
  - Omikron SR Interactive (web design, content creation, web hosting, and technical services),
  - Omikron Marketing Services (promotions, public relations, and publicity),
  - Avalanche of Fun Event Management,
  - ChinaRights (a literary rights agency for the Asian market)
  - Publisher, The Bakka Collection, a speculative fiction book publisher
  - Director of North American Operations, Posnayko, children's web publisher, Kiev, Ukraine
  - Director of Development, Toronto's Reel Asian International Film Festival
  - Communications Director, Move Sound + Design
  - Festival Manager, Sex and Death Short Film Festival,
  - Learn Publishing, Sales and Marketing Manager
  - Alive, Marketing Director
- General/Musson Publishing, Marketing Manager
- Raincoast Book Distribution, Publicity / Media Relations Manager
- Distican (Simon & Schuster), Publicity / Media Relations Manager
- Random House of Canada, Media Relations Officer
- Doubleday Book and Music Clubs, Marketing & Editorial Assistant
- Classic Bookshops (Chapters), Manager
- Writer, Producer & Publisher
  - Interviews, Trade Magazines and Newsletters (writer)
  - Publisher / Co-Publisher, book works
  - Executive Producer, audio works
- Event Management
  - PEN Benefit, Toronto Canada
  - Canadian Booksellers Association convention closing night festivities
  - Sex and Death Short Film Festival fundraisers
  - Annual Robbie Burns Bash (Toronto/Vancouver)

SELECT LIST OF PREVIOUS CLIENTS

"Sal Nensi was a resourceful and highly creative communications specialist, who contributed significantly to the launch and ultimate success of many books published by Simon & Schuster, as well as Alive Publishing. I highly recommend Sal to anyone interested in doing publicity directly or managing a team of individuals who deliver media results."

NOLAN MACHAN
Effective Online Communicator

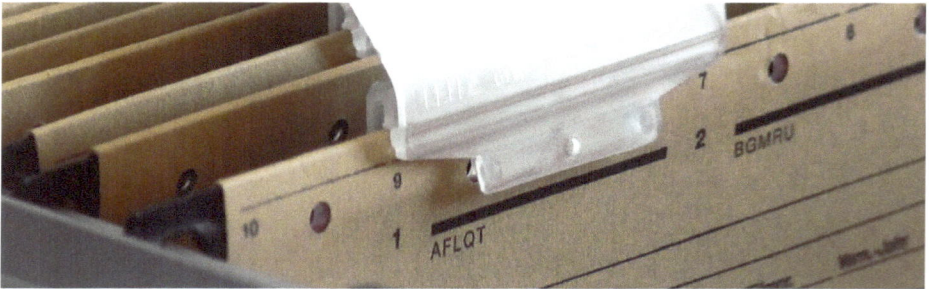

United Nations
United Nations Development Program (UNDP)
Aga Khan Development Network
Bell Canada
Rogers Communications
Star Trek: The Next Generation
Star Wars
Simon & Schuster
Hachette Book Group
Random House
Chronicle Books
McMaster University Press
Prentice Hall Canada
Roundhouse Publications

DLA Piper
Playmates Toys
Sex and Death Short Film Fest
Western Living Magazine
Association of Canadian Publishers
Canadian Booksellers Association
League of Canadian Poets
PEN Canada
Dorling Kindersley
Better Homes and Gardens
Canadian Geographic
Gamehole Con
Greenbrier Games
X-Bar Asia

EXPERIENCE (BY SKILL)

"I unwittingly fell into Salman's orbit and will be forever grateful I did. This is a professional at the top of his game with a breadth of experience Jules Verne couldn't dream up."

THOMAS DUNLOP
Navitas North America Student Recruitment Director

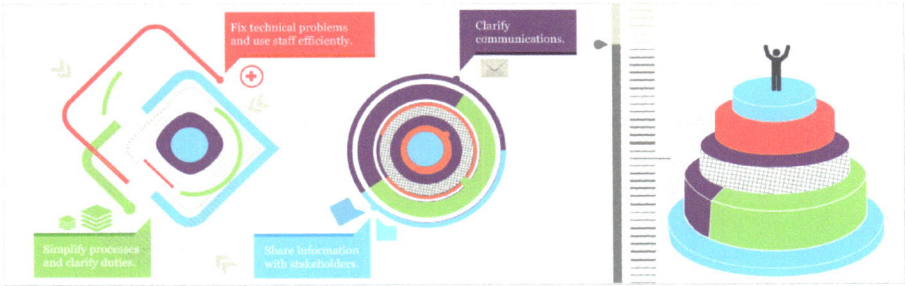

Strategic/Management Skills

• Hired, coached and motivated professional staff, team members, and freelance staff to help them achieve peak performances.
• Set, tracked, and maintained sales targets and spending budgets for clients, departments, and companies in order to increase profitability.
• Oversaw supplier relations for all purchases (materials and personnel) with budgets of up to $1 million.
• Evaluated, co-ordinated, and personally delivered charitable donations of money, product, and personnel.
• Assisted clients (NGOs, corporations, and individuals) in strategic project conceptualization (marketing, product development, event management) maximizing the business value (exposure, profit) created.
• Performed needs assessment, cost benefit, and risk analysis ensuring projects met client goals and budgets.
• Planned and organized the delegation of project tasks to team members (up to 300 persons) including setting of quality benchmarks and key decision points.
• Oversaw staff teams, internal and external suppliers, and clients' staff to ensure smooth communication and co-operation as project tasks were executed.

- Assessed project's success both externally for the client and internally for the corporation or department.
- (K Bez Creations) Assisted and nurtured the development of a consumer product company from the pre-concept stage. Once formed, acted as principal consultant on marketing, sales, distribution and business planning. Sourced manufacturers in Thailand, China, and Toronto and managed the packaging of the product across print and digital media.

Leadership Skills

- (Book Promoters Association of Canada) Took over the leadership of an ad hoc professional association for a two-year period. While President:
  - Reorganized and made constitutional reforms to strengthen its position in the industry;
  - Developed networking forums for national media, industry and association members—increasing membership by 250% and revenue by 300%;
  - Successfully lobbied for a series of government-funded workshops and forged international alliances throughout Europe and Asia.
- (The Omikron Group Inc.) Grew a part-time publicity company into an international operation of 25 freelancers in 5 countries (Canada, United States, China, England, and Australia). Consulting contracts and services covered a broad range of media, markets, and events focused primarily on the development of Canadian arts and culture. In 2001, Omikron's four divisions (Interactive, Marketing, Production, and Rights) were sold to different parties.
- (EBR Holdings, PTE, Ltd.) Managed and led teams of communication consultants, service providers, and creative artists in varied art forms from 3 to 500 team members for projects local to international.
- (UN Country Team, Nepal) Turned a small communications assessment consultancy into a full report encompassing all UN agencies operating in Nepal with input from all heads of agency, heads of communications, and each head of information technology. Highlights include saving agency projects tens of thousands of dollars; getting new projects green-lit using hitherto unknown internal county-team resources, and giving a series of lectures, talks, and informal workshops.

Creative Communications Skills

- Responsible for customer account management beginning with client acquisition, needs assessments, up- and cross-selling through to ensuring successful delivery of products and services including post sales customer support.
- Negotiated sales, distribution, and service contracts as well as international rights contracts.
- Researched, prepared, and presented corporate and department responses to external requests for proposals and quotes.
- (Random House / Bakka Books) Managed a media-starved and overlooked portfolio of genre writers. Raised the profile of the genre as a whole through a multidisciplinary luncheon series for authors and media. Built interest that led to the development of a widely distributed genre marketing kit. This kit garnered first-in-kind front page coverage for the portfolio and resulted in the publishing of a Canadian retrospective book of collected stories.
- (Raincoast Books) Improved operational and management processes in disparate business environments. Highlights include:
  - Holding a national series of interviews with major and minor media outlets, resulting in the introduction of tailored marketing vehicles which both streamlined publicity costs and dramatically increased media coverage;
  - Integrating real-time planning and distribution systems, which reduced turnaround from months to days, resulting in significant savings;
  - Tightly aligning marketing products to sales goals by introducing a very successful calendar-based sales tool to promote packages of new titles combined with stock overruns.

Teaching, Training & Lecturing

(Bubba Soft) While affiliated with a computer programmers' network:

- Identified an opportunity to provide educational software to the California Board of Education;
- Organized a small software company and facilitated a partnership with Commodore Computers;
- Launched two pilot projects focused on teaching ecological resource management.

(China Book Business Report) While at The Omikron Group:

- Identified a need for First World Media Practices to be taught to the Chinese book industry, specifically the book media and publishers
- Organized a series of lectures and presentations on:
  - Editorial Integrity
  - Press Release and Kit creation
  - Media List Management
  - Book Reviewer Relationship Management

(Seoul National University) While visiting South Korea asked to give a small series of lectures on Communications for business students.

- Created a curriculum, including lots of student participation
- Lectured and provided extra assistance for students in need
- Assisted a small group of students launch their own ventures

EXPERIENCE (BY POSITION)

"As soon as I began working with Salman, his years of experience in marketing, communications, and planning became obvious. His attention to the minutest detail drew out only the best ideas and concepts, whilst keeping the blood pumping in what (being the creative world) can dead-end with triviality. It is a huge task to organise so many individually creative minds (with all of their idiosyncrasies) and Salman was tireless in keeping us on track, as well as navigating what can be a convoluted and complex business."

MARTIN TREANOR
Author & Illustrator, Fall of Ancients

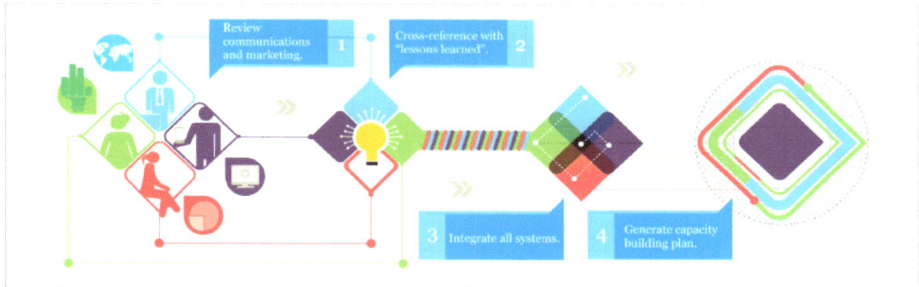

DRPZ, Business Development & Project Director
January 2020 ~ Present
Toronto

In January, 2020 Nensi joined a small group of communications consultants and publishing professionals as Head Project Catalyst with responsibilities for business development as well as sales, marketing and rights management.

- Business consulting for various business entities either based in or operating in Angola from property management to urban gardening and sales branding for fast moving consumer goods.
- Prompting a controversial publishing project focusing on meta fictional tri-planning that integrates sales, marketing and the IP itself. Favouring a new strategy that combines horizontal, vertical, and circular integration for the enjoyment of the audience from a project

that was both ontologically and holistically inspired.
• Recovery and rehabilitation in the public media sphere for individuals, companies and projects.
• Redefining the places and spaces clients work and live leads to productivity gains in all areas, both business and personal.

Nensi.com, Business Development & Project Director
January 2017 ~ Present
London * Toronto * Siem Reap

Nensi's work as an international communications manager has included

• brand development and management across multiple media channels;
• managing suppliers (including printers, software developers & distributors); and,
• hiring and supervising teams of writers, filmmakers, and web designers, and occasionally, close personal protection.

EBR Holdings Pte, Ltd (Singapore), Business Development & Project Director
January 2013 ~ December 2016
Client: Consultants, firms, experts, and suppliers (world-wide)

• In 2014, Nensi concluded almost two years of strategic, marketing, sales and contract negotiations with more than four dozen people and entities across multiple countries, languages, and cultures.
• Balancing each party's needs, wants, desires, talents, skills, and personalities—Nensi oversaw the creation of a cohesive and integrated network of communications strategists, marketers and managers aligned with a group of writers, designers, web, and other content generators. The new company works in a variety of markets and genres across the communications spectrum—words, visuals, audio, and video distributed in print, broadcast, and on the web.
• Simplified Systems: across the network there has been a significant drop in non-billable administrative hours per client.
• Coordinated Sales Force: the new network is big enough to warrant its own physical sales force.
• Self-Marketing: sharing talents/ideas across the network allowed many to improve their marketing/outbound communications.

• Private Labeling: network participants who keep their own name and branding have no barriers to adding additional services from the network to their own portfolio of offerings.
• Nensi's role as key architect led to the creation of a new type of firm that integrates communications specialists and content-generating creatives allowing better work to be produced faster, more easily, with less stress and
• budget saving across the whole network.

Beyond Reports, Business Development & Project Director
January 2002 ~ Present
International

Beyond Reports is a full-service network of professional project managers, editors, writers, designers, photographers, printing and publishing professionals, and web experts that understood the importance of clear design, excellent writing, thorough editing and accurate translation. Beyond Reports also provided capacity building and training in the areas of web and print publishing, media and communications.

• Directed hiring, staff management and project management, until successful client sign-off
• Assisted clients in identifying their communication desires, needs, and goals
• Walked clients through their initial decision-making process to ensure they chose the right communications vehicles for their goals
• Educated clients on how various communications vehicles work, the pros and cons of each, and the budgets and timelines of each in order to help them make informed decisions
• Coordinated Beyond Reports' team of talented freelancers to provide clients with the right people to help them achieve their goals, no matter the scale of the project

The Omikron Group Inc., Managing Director, Principal Agent & Publisher
January, 1988 ~ January, 2002
International

The Omikron Group included Omikron Marketing Services, Omikron Interactive, Avalanche of Fun event management, ChinaRights and

StoneFox / Bakka Publishing. Omikron provided consulting, marketing, publicity, promotions, and representation for authors, publishers, filmmakers, musicians, and other professionals in the entertainment industry.

- Managed client accounts, from acquisition of new clients through to successful completion of all existing contracts
- Devised and implemented publishing, web marketing, advertising, and media relations strategies for individuals, projects, books, CDs, book series, and publishers' imprints
- Consulted with publishers, government departments, and NGOs on numerous aspects of publishing, marketing, sales, and the impact of new technologies on the publishing industry
- Designed, planned, and executed North American marketing strategies for clients, including liaising with Viacom Canada, the City of Toronto, Kellogg's Canada, Blockbuster, and Famous Players
- Negotiated and advised on rights contracts for over 40 published and unpublished authors internationally, and represented mainland China rights for 30+ publishers
- Coordinated launches, public signings, parties, speaking engagements, and other publicity functions
- Prepared and managed the annual company budget
- Maintained publisher and media contacts through regular trips to Toronto, New York, Chicago, Beijing, Frankfurt, Vancouver, Victoria, Calgary, Edmonton, Seattle, and San Francisco.
- Actively participated in professional organizations BPAC, BPPA, SFWA, and CPRS.
- Organised all charitable donations (money, books, and personnel).

General/Musson Publishing, Marketing Manager
January 1996 ~ January 1997

General/Musson Publishing distributed for Virgin Publishing, STC (Stewart, Tabori & Chang), Grove Press, Hodder, Headline, and 20 other publishers, and was part of the Stoddart group of companies, a Canadian publishing group.

- Oversaw the media relations, marketing and sales departments for the trade, specialty markets, London Bridge, and library divisions, coordinating trade show appearances and all other promotions

• Implemented co-promotional marketing with distilleries, toy companies, packaged goods companies, music publishers, and motion picture studios, including Disney and Paramount
• Managed national (20+ city) media tours, coordinating accommodations, air travel, media, local media relations experts, and client escorts
• Coordinated the marketing department's involvement at the annual American Booksellers Association's convention (Chicago), the Canadian Booksellers Association's convention (Toronto and Vancouver), and two annual sales conferences (Toronto and Montreal)
• Coordinated U.S. marketing and media relations for five British publishers whom General represented in both Canada and the United States
• Served as a member of the web steering committee.

Raincoast Book Distribution, Media Relations Manager
January 1994 ~ January 1996

Raincoast Book Distribution, the largest publishing and distribution company in western Canada, represented Chronicle Books, Bloomsbury, Pavilion, Lonely Planet, and 50 other publishers.

• Generated media exposure (television, radio, newspaper, periodical) for all titles, authors, and genres in the publishing and distribution divisions, and provided corporate and divisional public relations
• Prepared and managed the annual media relations budget
• Saved thousands of dollars per month and hundreds of human resource-hours per year by streamlining the number of free books mailed annually, from 10,000 units to fewer than 3,000
• Increased review coverage by 45% in the first year, and by an additional 65% in the second year
• Expanded media contact database by 300%
• Managed the media relations department (up to 6 staff)

Distican (Simon & Schuster), Media Relations Manager
January 1993 ~ January 1994

Distican distributed for Simon & Schuster, Macmillan Reference, Charles Scribner's Sons, Free Press, Atheneum, and Pocket Books, and is the Canadian distributor for all Viacom/Paramount Publishing imprints.

- Generated media exposure (television, radio, newspaper, periodical) and other forms of media relations for all titles, authors, and genres in the trade division
- Managed corporate and divisional public relations
- Established and supervised the setup of the trade-media relations department
- Increased the number of media contacts by 50%

Random House of Canada, Media Relations Officer
1992 ~ 1993

In addition to its own Canadian publishing program, Random House is the distributor for 50 imprints from its UK and US divisions, and is one of the largest trade publishing houses in the world.

- Devised and implemented media relations strategies for the publishing and distribution divisions, with special responsibility for the Ballantine Group (Ballantine, Del Rey, Fawcett, House of Collectibles, Ivy, and One World), Arrow, Legend Paperbacks, RH Reference, RH Electronic Publishing, and TSR imprints
- Attracted media coverage by creating dynamic press kits and releases
- Coordinated book launch parties, public signings, presentations, and other public functions
- Managed national media tours (4-12 cities) and personally guided celebrities through intensive public appearance tours
- Negotiated the sale of first and second serial rights to magazines, newspapers, and other organisations

Doubleday Book and Music Clubs, Marketing & Editorial Assistant
1991

(The Doubleday Book Club, The Literary Guild, The Science Fiction Book Club, and four other clubs.) Doubleday is the largest book club company in the world.

- Assessed manuscripts for acquisition and marketability
- Created advertising copy for book selections in monthly mailings
- Wrote Editorial Letters for various monthly mailings
- Supervised the design and layout of the monthly mailings

- Liaised with the publisher representative regarding possible new acquisitions and continued marketing of titles already acquired
- Created marketing analysis for the President, and Director of Marketing
- Shared responsibility for seeing manuscripts safely from the acquisition stage, through layout, design, and production, to marketing and sales

Chapters, Manager
1984 ~ 1992

Manager (1988), Full-time (summers), Part-time (Classic Bookshops); (Chapters, Coles, Book Company, Classic Bookshops, W.H.Smith, Celebration, Paperchase, and Smithbooks.) Chapters was Canada's largest bookstore chain.

- Implemented new special order and returns procedures thereby increasing efficiency
- Responsible for the screening and training of over 40 employees
- Increased sales by accurately tailoring existing marketing strategies to meet the needs of the local clientele
- Developed cooperative ventures with local high schools
- Evaluations consistently in the top ten percent
- Responsible for employee relations and customer service in addition to marketing, inventory control, budgeting, sales management, and for increasing sales

PORTFOLIO

Hewadwal (Kabul) Project | Moving Mountains (Dushanbe) | Posnayko (Kyiv) | Nepal Information Platform | Tajikistan NDS Translation | National Poetry Month (Canada) | "Start with Why" (New York) | PEN Canada Benefit (Toronto) | TEGG, Inc. (International)

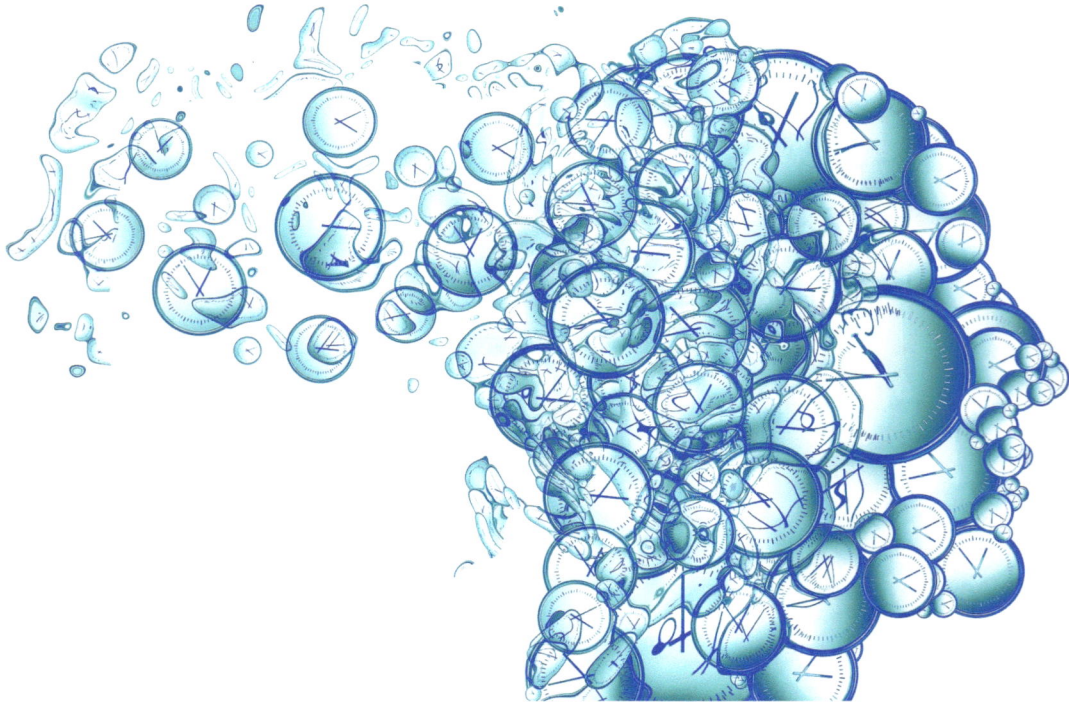

HEWADWAL (KABUL) PROJECT

"These are not photographs. These are Art."

WAHEED KHAN
Director, Hewadwal Group

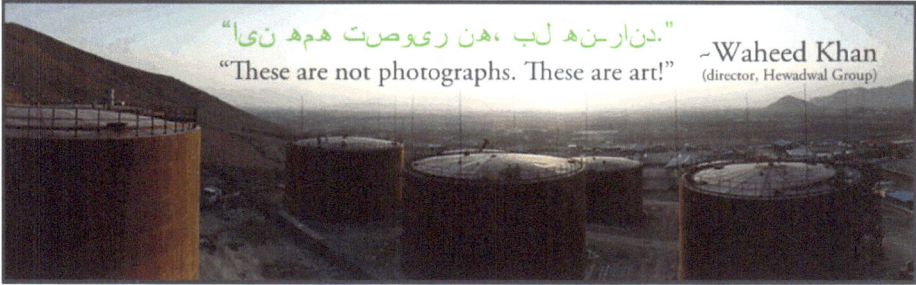

"این همه تصویر هن، بل هنراند."
"These are not photographs. These are art!" ~Waheed Khan
(director, Hewadwal Group)

2008

In 2008, Nensi travelled to Afghanistan to prepare promotional materials for the Hewadwal Group. This involved

- navigating in English, Pashto, and Dari for communications and travel arrangements;
- visiting completed and in-progress construction sites with local staff, armed security guards, and a photographer; and
- producing photographs to be used when bidding for future projects and applying for grants.

The resulting marketing materials have enabled Hewadwal to win construction contracts and grants for projects throughout Afghanistan.

MOVING MOUNTAINS (DUSHANBE)

*". . . many of your recommendations will be
part of the transition process . . ."*

MARTIN HART-HANSEN
UN Nepal Resident Coordinator's office

2006

In 2006, Nensi and his team coordinated the efforts of 20+ agencies and produced the annual appeal document for the United Nations Country Team in Tajikistan, which involved:

- working from reports in multiple formats in both Tajik and Russian from numerous UN programmes;
- leading the project in-country and improving workflow to reduce consulting time from three months to two weeks; and
- writing, editing, and designing the 60-page final product in Russian and English.

Our report was effective and engaging, and the savings realised allowed the UN to produce a Russian edition without an increase in the base budget.

For more, please visit UNDP Tajikistan (https://www.tj.undp.org/).

POSNAYKO (KYIV)

"His abilities . . . have created an indelible impression."

MAYA STEPANOVA
Director, Posnayko

2002

In 2002, Nensi designed a multifaceted advertising campaign with a budget of CAD$250,000 for the North American launch of Posnayko, an English-learning website based in Ukraine. This involved:

- travelling to Ukraine for organisational meetings (which required learning basic Russian);
- producing online promotions, ads on public transit and in major periodicals, as well as the distribution of thousands of Posnayko branded magazines, stickers, and postcards;
- coordinating readings in Toronto libraries, a presence at trade shows, a direct-mail campaign and delivery of the Posnayko message to children's media; and,
- participating in the Word On The Street festival (including having an elaborate mascot costume made and hiring storytellers to act as Posnayko).

Nensi's promotion of the event reached Posnayko's target audience, making it possible for the firm to gauge the market and plan further actions in other countries.

NEPAL INFORMATION PLATFORM

"Salman was hired to do a detailed review of the UN Nepal website and provide recommendations as to how it could be improved both from a design perspective as well as a service provision perspective. He did a very detailed and thorough analysis and provided a wealth of options. He went beyond his terms of reference and put in many more hours and days than agreed since he wanted to make sure we got the full picture.
Highly Recommended."

MARTIN HART-HANSEN
CEO and Strategic Planning Advisor at United Nations Volunteers

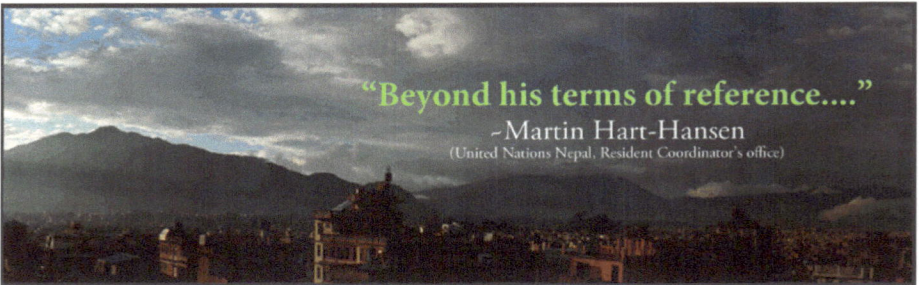

"Beyond his terms of reference...."
~Martin Hart-Hansen
(United Nations Nepal, Resident Coordinator's office)

2008

In 2008, Nensi recommended improvements to the website of the UN Nepal Resident Coordinator's Office. Remotely managing a team of consultants, Nensi:

- reviewed 10+ existing in-country UN websites;
- personally led in-country meetings with 30 heads of agencies and over 60 communications and IT professionals; and
- produced a 125-page report detailing a strategy for improving both the existing site and internal communications of the UN Nepal Resident Coordinator's Office.

Nensi also showed the UN how to save time and money by coordinating and integrating existing systems instead of purchasing new, expensive ones.

TAJIKISTAN NDS TRANSLATION

"Salman's speed sometimes takes your breath away. His globalised team and style of work boost your creativity. They bring you real fun plus high-quality products."

THEKLA KELBERT
UN Country Team Coordinator

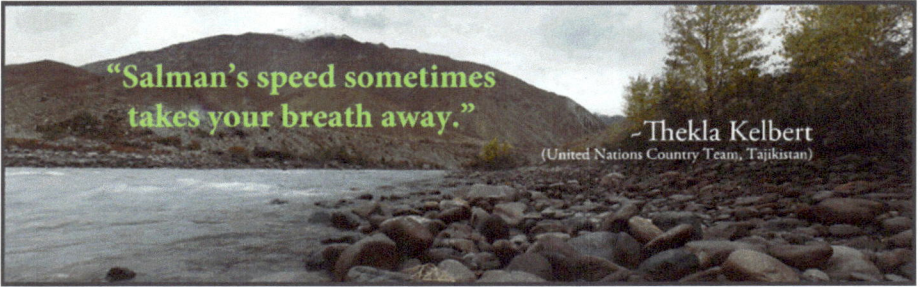

"Salman's speed sometimes takes your breath away."
~Thekla Kelbert
(United Nations Country Team, Tajikistan)

2005

In 2005, Nensi directed the translation of the Tajik Government's National Development Strategy, an integral part of Tajikistan's endeavour to achieve the UN Millennium Development Goals (MDG) by 2015. The 100-page report was to be translated from Russian to English, so that non-Russian-speaking experts could access the document and give their input. The situation did not allow for a predictable start date for the project; the submitted document was 40% longer than expected and the deadline for a translated, proofed and typeset deliverable had to remain at seven days. Accomplishing this task required:

- preparing the necessary materials so that the document could be translated, edited, proofed, and typeset as quickly as possible;
- coordinating a team of 12 experienced translators, editors, and designers based in three countries; and
- ensuring efficient communication and workflow in order to deliver a clear, attractive English-language version of the report.

Despite the uncertain start time and the project's unexpected size, Nensi's organisation and preparation allowed him and his team to deliver a high-quality product within six days, a full day in advance of the deadline, and under budget.

NATIONAL POETRY MONTH (CANADA)

"I'm not sure which was more astonishing, the breadth and creativity of your plan, or the fact that you pulled it off to perfection."

GORDON PLATT
Head, Writing and Publishing Section, Canada Council for the Arts

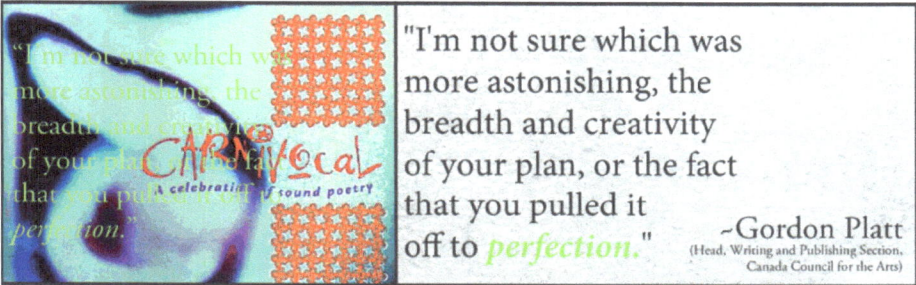

"I'm not sure which was more astonishing, the breadth and creativity of your plan, or the fact that you pulled it off to *perfection*." ~Gordon Platt (Head, Writing and Publishing Section, Canada Council for the Arts)

2000

In 1999 and 2000, Nensi led the media campaigns for the League of Canadian Poets' National Poetry Month. Nensi:

- produced press kits and email releases that were disseminated to over 1000 media outlets;
- motivated hundreds of bookstores, libraries, publishers, and many other organisations to hold performances, poetry readings, and contests; and,
- co-published and acted as executive producer for "Carnivocal", an anthology of Canadian sound poetry.

The publicity achieved national coverage of National Poetry month in television, radio, and print media, aiding the league's goal of promoting poetry among the Canadian audience.

"START WITH WHY" (NEW YORK)

"Thank you, Sal. I appreciate your amazing energy to want to share the Why with as many people as possible. Very special to have you be a part of this movement. With great appreciation."

SIMON SINEK
Author of *Start With Why*

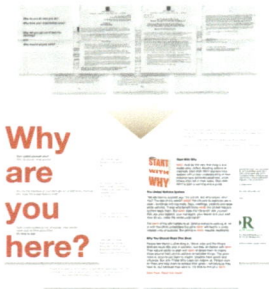

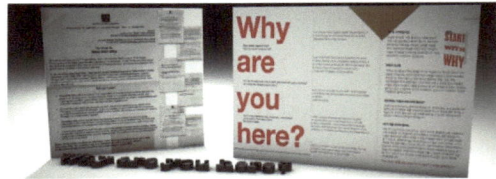

2010

In 2010, Nensi identified a pressing need within the United Nations and donated his services to deliver Simon Sinek's inspiring analysis of leadership and motivation, Start with WHY, into the hands of 135 UN resident representatives and the heads of 32 global agencies. He then:

- collaborated with the author to upgrade press materials into effective and arresting communication pieces;
- sourced donations of writing, editing, translation, design, layout & production services; and
- produced a Korean-language version of the material that was presented to UN Secretary-General Ban Ki-moon.

Nensi's donation increased interest in the author's message, his lectures and workshops.

PEN CANADA BENEFIT (TORONTO)

"A giant thank you."
ANN IRELAND

President, PEN Canada

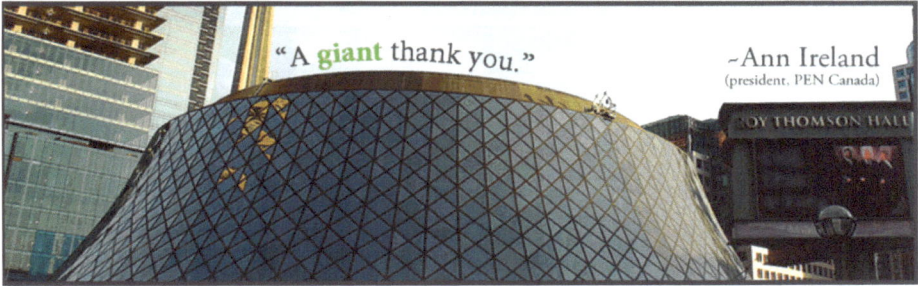

1999

In 1999, Nensi led the organisation of PEN Canada's annual benefit. This involved:

- translating the ideas of the benefit's organisers into achievable plans and disseminating press and promotional materials about the upcoming event;
- coordinating the efforts and needs of 150+ volunteers and staff across 14 committees, and managing the logistics for nearly 30 restaurants and wineries; and,
- providing logistical support for a 90-minute performance, an art installation, a food festival, a wine tasting, and a silent auction.

Nensi's adroit event management and quick problem solving on several fronts resulted in attendance of 1000+ guests and increased exposure for PEN Canada.

TEGG, INC. (INTERNATIONAL)

"For Sal: 'You wade through shit and then you find a Johna?'
—W.S. Burroughs.
Many, many thanks for everything."

WILL SELF
Author of *Great Apes* (Grove Atlantic)

2010~2018

In 2010 planning started for a publishing and media entity operating globally. The project officially launched in October, 2015 after a series of market tests. The entity boasted 12 publishing lines and 11 media divisions operating as the Onder Media Group. At its height there were 500+ creative persons connected to the network with works being produced in multiple formats and languages. Nensi's main areas of responsibility were:

- logistics management
- book design
- creative consulting
- worldbuilding
- meta / trans fictional connectivity
- and integrating sales, marketing, rights, audience building and audience-keeping.

Nensi's leadership skills helped realize stronger story settings with solid ties to audience engagement without compromising on fan-service. Check out the book *Clouds in My Coffee* for more details.

"Your brain is operating on a level most mortals don't grok. Some people MULTItask . . . you SIMULtask. It's a beautiful thing."

DAVE ROBISON
Vice President, The Ed Greenwood Group

WRITING: BUSINESS, COMMUNICATIONS, MEMOIRS, FOOD & TRAVEL

Memoirs | Business | Fiction | Publications | Read about Salman's adventures in food, travel, and his interviews with Barker, Brooks, and Takei

MEMOIRS

How to Steal a Rickshaw

Cooking yaks, getting swindled, and avoiding uniformed twits across the "other Asia" and around the world.

by Salman A. Nensi with photographs by Oliver K. L. Strong and others

"The fact that 'Stealing a Rickshaw' is not a posthumous story about Sal clearly shows that he is a man who 'really knows where his towel is.'"
DILEEP RANGAN

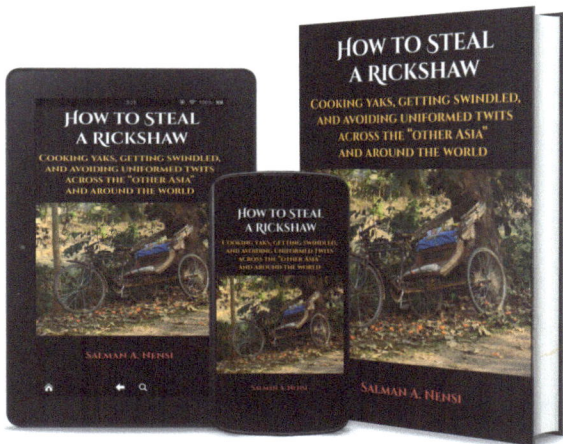

Storyteller Salman Nensi shares 40 years of stories collected from dozens of countries: food, spectacle, villains, and a few heroes in his audio memoirs: *How To Steal a Rickshaw* which crafts a strange and sometimes beautiful vision of our world: a world peered at through the lens of a communications professional working in places and spaces both exotic and sometimes just plain weird.

  • "*Seemed like a good idea at the time*," said Nensi explaining how he and Strong ended up teaching their cooking teacher how to make pancakes out of pig feed in Bhutan.

How to Steal a Rickshaw is part travelogue, part culinary exploration, and part social commentary—Nensi's wry humour and off kilter way of looking at life will have you laughing and scratching your head at what goes on in the big wide world.

It is this unique insight on the weird and wonderful that also helped author Martin Treanor lay down the Fall of Ancients, a trilogy of novels telling a bizarre story of humanity—from 26,500 BP to thousands of years in the future. The first novel drops Fall 2022.

Audiobooks, podcasts, and illustrated transcript available at Zariqa.com.

⁂

"Too Late Now . . . Pass The Kebabs!"
Afghan deep-fried goat, Nepali yak, Tibetian momos and other delicious adventures.

by Salman A. Nensi with photographs by Oliver K. L. Strong

"'Too Late Now . . . Pass The Kebabs!' is filled with humour, joie de vivre, and unvarnished unbiased observations of the features of our world—both good and bad."
STEVE BOWDEN

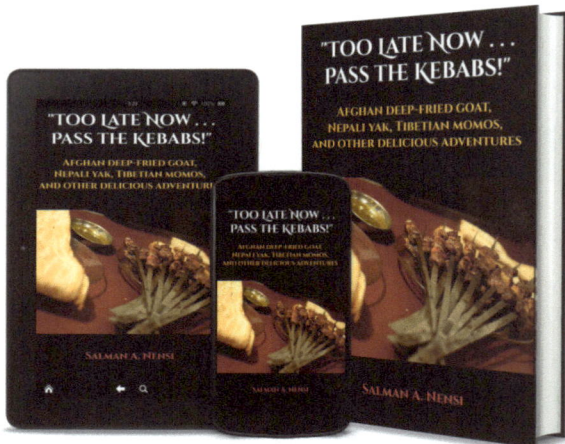

The mission to find and eat the most local of local dishes around the world has taken me to some exotic places filled with amazing people and brilliantly delicious foods. For more about the travels you can listen to the *How to Steal a Rickshaw* podcast but for a more culinary romp through the cuisines of the Other Asia we present: "Too Late Now . . . Pass The Kebabs!"

• *"It wasn't my fault,"* said Nensi when asked about the night he went out to meet the 'Jim Belushi' of Dhaka for a drink and ended up

coming home at 3am with a rickshaw but no driver.
- *"Too late now...Pass the kebabs!"* is what Strong suggests you think while eating lunch in local, unsecured, non UN registered restaurants in Kabul.
- Useful phrases and translations:
  - *Man gooftam konkretna* is Tajik for *"You've messed up... completely."*
  - *Man Ba Quomandan astam* is Dari (Afghan) for *"I'm with The Commander!"*
  - The word Inshallah is oft translated to mean, *"When god wishes it."* This word is better understood by the colloquial term, *"Yeah, right!"*

"Too Late Now . . . Pass The Kebabs!"—the companion cookbook to How to Steal a Rickshaw—brings the reader even deeper into Nensi's travels whilst maintaining his wry humour and off kilter way of looking at life will have you laughing and scratching your head at what goes on in the big wide world. It's got recipes too!

It is this unique insight on the weird and wonderful that also helped author Martin Treanor lay down the Fall of Ancients, a trilogy of novels telling a bizarre story of humanity—from 26,500 BP to thousands of years in the future. The first novel drops Fall 2022.

Audiobook, podcast and illustrated transcript available at Zariqa.com.

BUSINESS

Ontological Integration
21st Century Communication Priorities for Organisations

by Salman A. Nensi and Beyond Reports Consultants

"Salman did a very detailed and thorough analysis and provided a wealth of options. He went beyond his terms of reference and put in many more hours and days than agreed since he wanted to make sure we got the full picture. Highly Recommended."

MARTIN HART-HANSEN
CEO and Strategic Planning Advisor at United Nations Volunteers

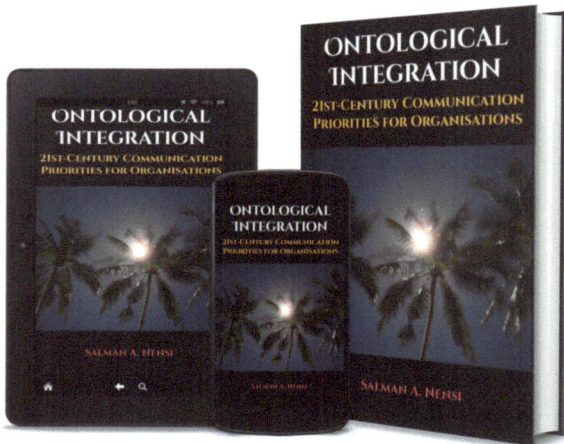

This is a handout any organization (or person) can use to get themselves into a proper, well-thought-out plan—a distilled version of the book. Communications touch every aspect of your world, if you'd like anyone to listen to you . . . more so if you'd like them to then do something (click, like, share, buy). Your communication plan is vital; and this plan must prompt others to take action.

We live in a world where impressions, good and bad, are made in a fraction of a second, and effective communication is essential to deliver your message to the right people. Following is a list of Nensi's insights and immediate recommendations, which can enhance an organisation's ability to communicate globally and better achieve its ultimate goals.

Communications Priorities:

- Priority #1: Capacity Assessment
- Priority #2: Capacity Building—Internal
- Priority #3: Sales and Marketing—Outbound
- Priority #4: Ontology
- Some Ideas and Tools
- Conclusion

Imagine how such a "system refresh" will increase morale, efficiency, and accuracy, while freeing up time and funds for the organisation, its staff, and the work they do.

Booklet available for free at Zariqa.com.

The Past Be But Prologue?
The Curriculum Vitae of Salman A. Nensi

by Salman A. Nensi

"From one believer in the magic to another."

TERRY BROOKS
Author of The Sword of Shannara (Del Rey)

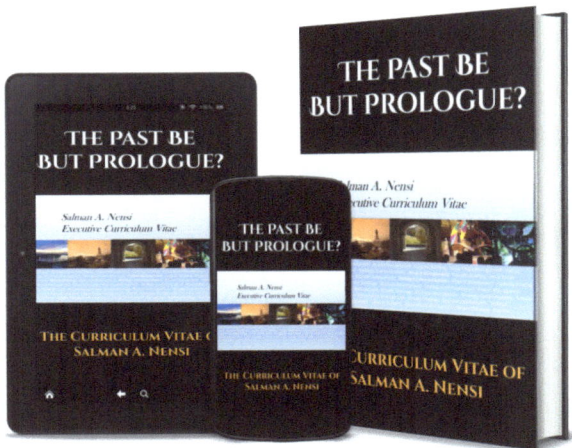

For over three decades Nensi has coordinated all aspects of message delivery, from brand development to internal reporting, for clients around the world. As an innovative thinker, he finds solutions to problems that others consider intractable. Having worked in over thirty countries with differing languages, cultures, and sensitivities, Nensi has a network extending across more than ninety countries. This range enables deep insight into each project he tackles. Nensi's holistic, thoughtful, and well-planned contributions lead to streamlined and effective communications.

Clients say Nensi finds solutions where none were thought to exist and ensures a job gets done efficiently and properly. He is a good facilitator, with a specialization in getting the most out of creative individuals who may not always work effectively in the corporate world. Nensi also has over twenty years experience in publishing, writing, editing, production, design, distribution, and new technologies.

One of the things Nensi loves is travelling: "I have been fortunate enough to have clients and work that have allowed me the freedom to travel and this is a great joy." Another interest is food and cooking. His travels have led to fabulous days of market shopping and cooking in the most amazingly bizarre kitchens in Bhutan, Nepal, Tibet, Bangladesh, Korea, and China.

Available in digital, paperback and hardcover at Zariqa.com.

Why You Fail . . .
Cuz you lazy and don't listen! Lessons learned from more than 30 years of gits and twits!

by Salman A. Nensi
▲Includes excerpts from emails, photographs, illustrations, scans, and contemporaneous notes from journals.

"Sal brings a great deal of energy, a can-do attitude, creativity, passion and out-of-the-box thinking to projects. He's also fun to work with."

MICHAEL KOVRIG
Senior Adviser, North East Asia at International Crisis Group

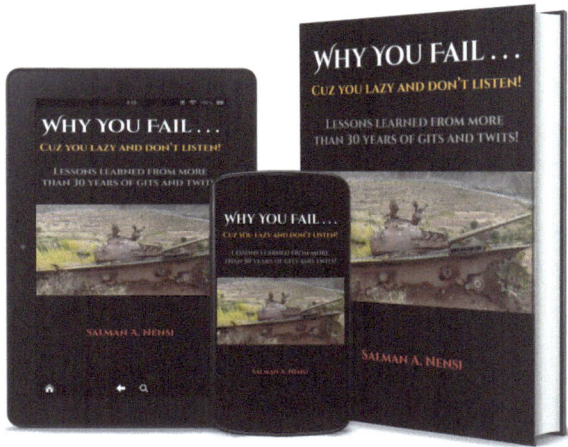

It's not hard to understand why most people and their projects fail: It's more fun to talk about something than to get down to the hard slog of actually doing something. After 30+ years of working with hundreds of clients—from high-end international law firms and NGOs like the UN, to individual authors and artists, to small business owners in dozens of countries, Nensi says the answer became obvious: "Doing is work. Learning is work. No one wants to do extra work. Above all else, that is why people fail!"

Nensi's irreverent humour and breezy style will have readers crying, laughing, and looking for the nearest wall upon which to bash their heads as he reviews decades of twits and gits who simply didn't listen:

- paid for plans and then ignored them
- did what they wanted (just *cuz*)
- did inane and occasionally criminal things (bribery, plagiarism, customer swindling, graft, assault, tax scams, corruption, solicitation, bizarre hires and fires)
- said things (lies, racism, sexism, misogyny).

Each tale ends with Lessons Learned (don't be lazy) and Things To Do (listen and learn).

Why You Fail . . . is an easy to read, funny, and poignant look at the realities of taking an idea and breathing life into it.

Why You Fail . . . workbook edition includes a simple two-page marketing and communications plan that can be used by *anyone* willing to listen, learn, and actually do the work. Also includes checklists, links to additional resources and Nensi's own guidance to help you and your project succeed.

Available in digital, paperback and hardcover at Zariqa.com.

* * *

Clouds in My Coffee
The Spectacularly Explosive Failures of
It Seemed A Good Idea at the Time

by EBR Holdings with Salman A. Nensi

▲Includes excerpts from emails, photographs, illustrations, scans, and contemporaneous notes from journals, court documents, and access to a searchable database of 10,000+ emails and documents.

"Sal is like a horror film! He absolutely terrifies you at first with his bold, creative approaches to problems. Then he chases you around until you see why you should do what he suggests. Next, he dispatches quickly but efficiently. AND it all works out really well in the end!"

CRAIG RINTOUL
Producer-Writer-Director at Kushog View Productions

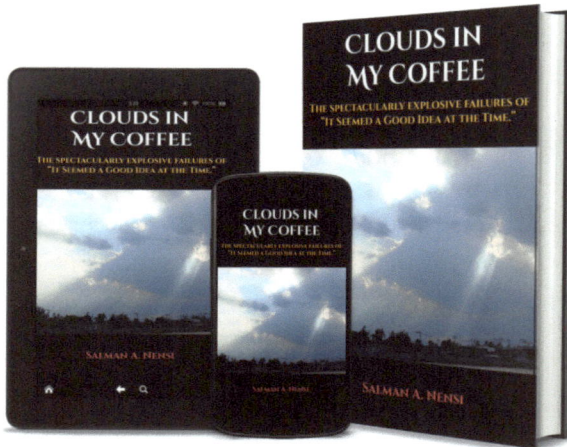

Consultants are humans . . . we too dream but sometimes dreams are only clouds . . .

For over 60 years the consultants at EBR have worked with clients from 135+ countries, in various fields, industries including the United Nations and other NGOs, governmental ministries and departments, companies, firms, and corporations. Adding up the number of years each EBR consultant has been helping others get their messages across . . . well it's in the 1,000s of hours.

Here then is the EBR cumulative wisdom on clients as we examine the role of communications consultants in the 21st century using a fictitious example to assist in more broadly understanding the complexities of message management and client relations in this new, ever changing comms-landscape.

This case study then examines the failure of a good idea at the time to achieve the plans set forth for it and finds lessons to be learned from each failure. We also examine the deeper communications issue of message transference and the various methods used to achieve message incorporation in the recipient as the single biggest consultant-side issue. Additional concepts examined include organisational behaviour, human group dynamics, peer pressure in professional situations, messaging in the split-second universe, and the role of the Reagan/Thatcherite-individual in 21st-century creative collaborations.

The study follows, step-by-step, the creation of a plan and the unanticipated need to consistently rework the plan as the client as with so many, also over-estimated their own brand, their own skills, their own network of friends and family that WILL actually help instead of becoming energy vampires draining both client and project. With a significant miscalculation of drawing power the client's professional friends too turn out to have similar issues, have no drawing power of their own, but were also suffering from a common ailment with creatives: hypersensitivity and inability to take constructive criticism ("*Precious Snowflake Syndrome*"). A team was never going to be possible . . . the journey to that realization in six steps . . .

The Journey; in Six Parts . . .

1. In the Beginning . . .
    • Researching the Dream
    • Failure
    • Solution

2. A Good Idea at the Time . . .
    • Sure . . . invite your friends
    • Failure
    • Solution

3. The Road to Hell is Paved with Snowflakes . . .
   • Are you sure? Open Call for Members
   • Failure
   • Solution: The Great Culling

4. The Great Culling: Won't someone rid me of these non-performing professionals?
   • The Plan is again reworked
   • Failure
   • Solution: Time to be alone.

5. Nothing to See Here: The great alleged #MeToo incident
   • Multiple allegations
   • Failure
   • Solution: Shut Down

6. Dishonourable Dismount: The art of backstabbing those that saved you.
   • It's not me doing this to you . . .
   • Failure
   • Solution: Client reneges on all promises; hires lawyers and denies payments for work done.

The role of suppliers and other third parties will also be touched upon.

Available in digital, paperback and hardcover at Zariqa.com.

FICTION

First We Take Jerusalem (as author)

King William reclaims the British Empire in the 21st Century A trilogy:
Jerusalem | Retribution | Empire

by Salman A. Nensi with Greig José & Kurt José

"As soon as I began working with Salman, his years of experience in marketing, communications, and planning became obvious. His attention to the minutest detail drew out only the best ideas and concepts, whilst keeping the blood pumping in what (being the creative world) can dead-end with triviality. It is a huge task to organise so many individually creative minds (with all of their idiosyncrasies) and Salman was tireless in keeping us on track, as well as navigating what can be a convoluted and complex business."

MARTIN TREANOR
Author & Illustrator, Fall of Ancients

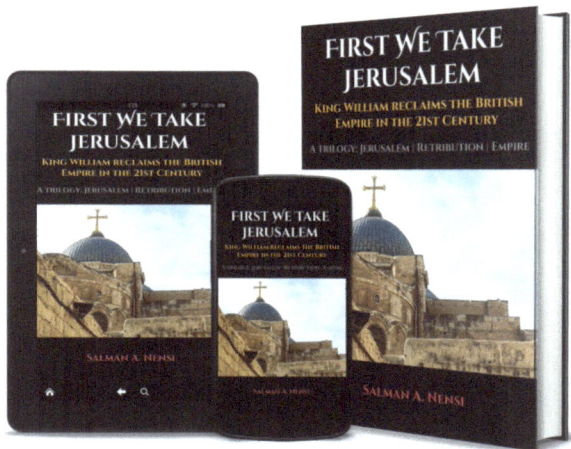

Queen Elizabeth II dies at 102. Charles has retired, so the crown passes to his son, William. At this time the world is in chaos. Putin, at 76, is more ambitious than ever. Two American presidential candidates have been assassinated in the same year. During William's coronation, Putin annexed Latvia. A year later William and his closest friend talk about how the world was better when it was ruled by the United Kingdom. After a pause . . . William asks his friend, "Why don't we take it back?"

"Take what back?"

"The World."

There is a pause as both men consider the weight of those two words.

"Well, your highness, if we are to take back the world . . . first we take Jerusalem. Here's why . . ."

Available soon from Zariqa.com.

Fall of Ancients (as producer and co-creator)
When the past and future collide—the truth will be revealed. A trilogy:
Arcadia's End | Deceit of Ages (published first) | Destruction Seed

Novels and short works by Martin Treanor

"You've got great shit going on in your head . . .
it's fucking brilliant, I love it."

MARTIN TREANOR
Creative Partner

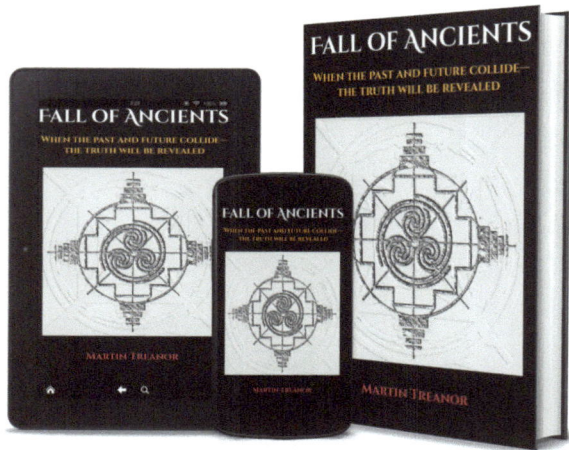

At the end of an ancient Glorious Era, an apprentice Sophist and a tribal guide attempt to ensure Knowledge—the wisdom of the ages—is maintained in the aftermath of an unavoidable and catastrophic comet impact. 12,900 years later, a conspiracy blogger and a science magazine editor uncover the malign machinations of a clandestine organization bent on global domination. Their combined efforts, both ancient and in the present day, culminate thousands of years in the future, when a lone scholar has noticed that the passage to universal Balance has slowed, the upshot of which might halt the continuous Cycle of Universes.

For more please visit:

- FallOfAncients.com
- MartinTreanor.com
- ANiceCuppaTea.com

Available soon from FireHornetCodex.com.

⚜

Star Trek: A Mugato in the Hand is Worth!?
(as storyteller)

Four bits of fan-fiction set in the original Star Trek universe based on the homages granted by the talented writers and fans that helped create and shape this optimistic view of humanity's future.

by Salman A. Nensi

"Sal, thank you for your company."
JOHN DE LANCIE
Actor, Q on Star Trek: The Next Generation

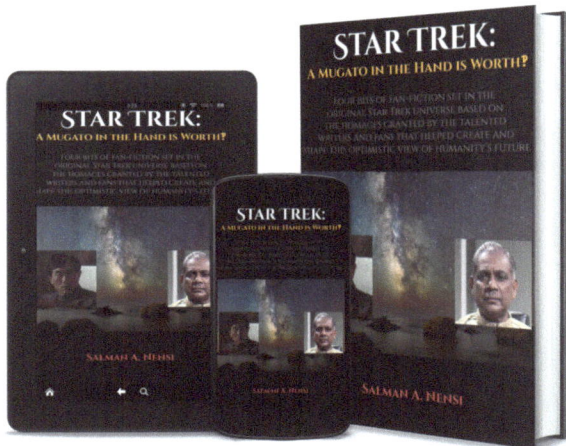

Somewhere in the distant past that was the '80s Nensi met two authors, Garfield and Judith Reeves-Stevens. They bonded over their interest in genre and *Starlog* magazine. The Reeves-Stevens' later went on to write a *Star Trek* book and Nensi was to be their research assistant looking up arcane bits of *Star Trek* lore long before the Internet became a thing. This led to Nensi writing a column for the *Star Trek Communicator* magazine for over nine years, each month interviewing authors and actors. Author Michael Jan Friedman named an interstellar phenomenon after Nensi in his book *Reunion* and many years later in the 2009 reboot, Nensi's name appeared as the first name of an admiral which, due to the vagaries of time-travelling aliens, led to a previously unnamed character in the 1966 original television series also getting "Nensi" as his first name.

Here then are the four stories, one based on each homage, with thanks to the authors, fans and all the entertainment creatives who have kept the adventure alive for more than fifty years.

In the Original Timeline:

1. "Star Trek: A Mugato in the Hand is Worth!?"
2. "Star Trek: Bolian Pastries"
3. "Star Trek: Explosions in Time"

In the Kelvin (reboot) Timeline:

4. "Star Trek: Between Logic and Claws"

Audiobook, digital, paperback and hardcover available soon from Zariqa.com.

PUBLICATIONS

"Sal is that rarest of things: a publisher brimming with creativity and passion, who understands real-world marketing and satisfying the consumer, and how those best mesh with, and enhance, published products."
ED GREENWOOD
Freelance Writing and Game Design

PUBLICATIONS
(as writer, editor)

• W(h)ither Gutenberg: Technology and Publishing, Association of Canadian Publishers, co-author, 2000
  ◦ This report acts as an e-book primer detailing the technical issues surrounding e-book creation, including formats, security, dissemination, and digital rights management. The report also discusses e-marketing tools; selling e-books to bookstores and readers and how the electronic world may affect author royalties, bookstore discounts and, ultimately, ways in which the publishing model will be transformed.

• Scotch: A Journal, StoneFox Publishing, co-author, 2000
  ◦ "A malt whisky tasting journal—what a great idea!" ~Ian Rankin

• The Changing Diet, Aga Khan Foundation / Toronto, editor, 1991

• Women's Faith, Real Stories, ARIS Community Development and Investment Agency, editor, 2006

NEWSPAPERS AND MAGAZINES (writer)

Various articles and celebrity interviews with authors including Nick Bantock, Clive Barker, George Takei, David Prowse and more.

- *Arirang magazine*
- *Bold magazine*
- *Cryptych magazine*
- *Edmonton Journal*
- *Excalibur*
- *Financial Post*
- *Latidos magazine*
- *Montréal Gazette*
- *NOW Magazine*
- *Seoul lifestyle & culture magazine*
- *The Archivist*
- *Travel Life magazine*

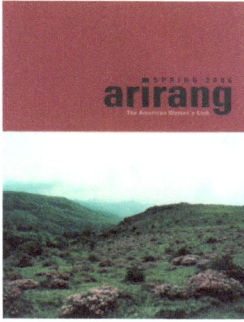

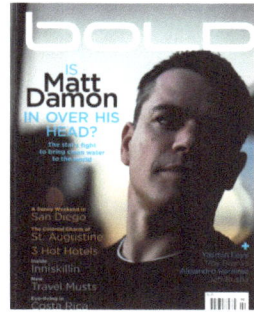

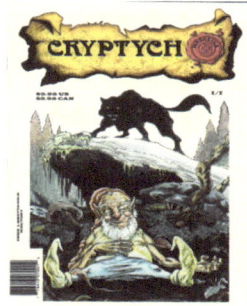

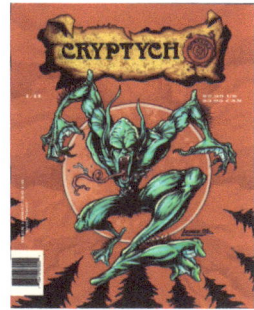

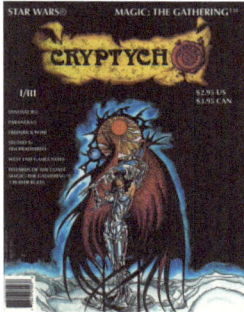

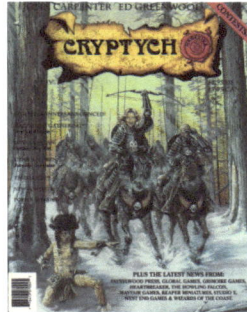

TRADE & FAN MAGAZINES AND NEWSLETTERS (writer)

- *The Sci-Fi Channel magazine*
- *The Star Trek Communicator*
- *The Star Wars Fan Club magazine*
- *China Book Business Report*
- *Network News*
- *Quill and Quire*
- *Reader's Showcase*

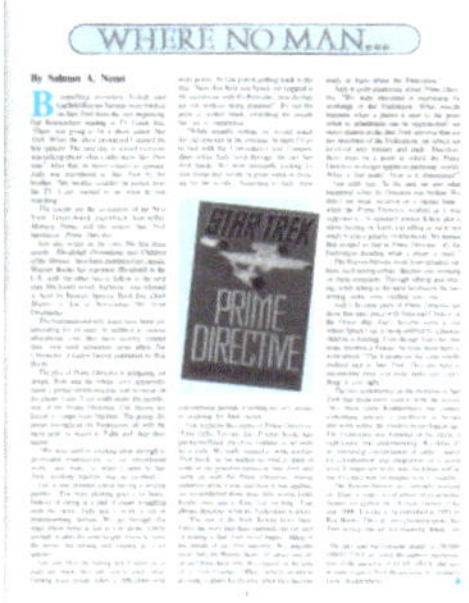

WHERE NO MAN...

By Salman A. Nensi

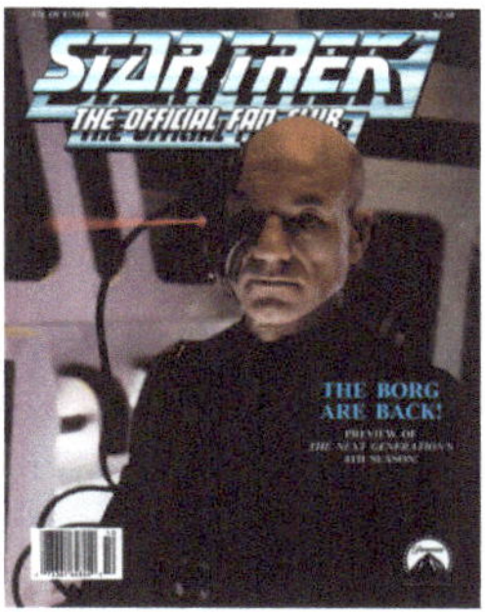

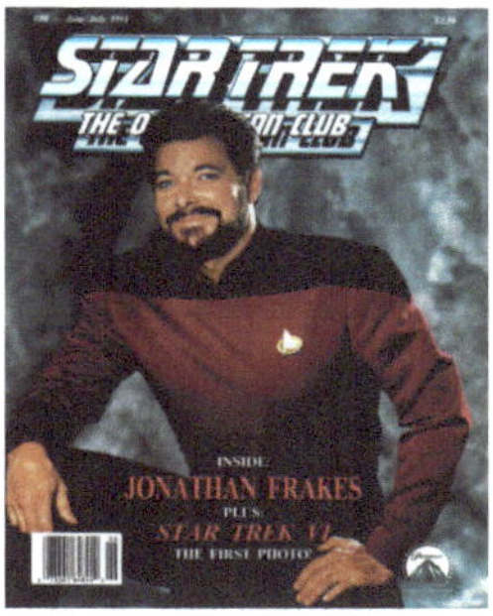

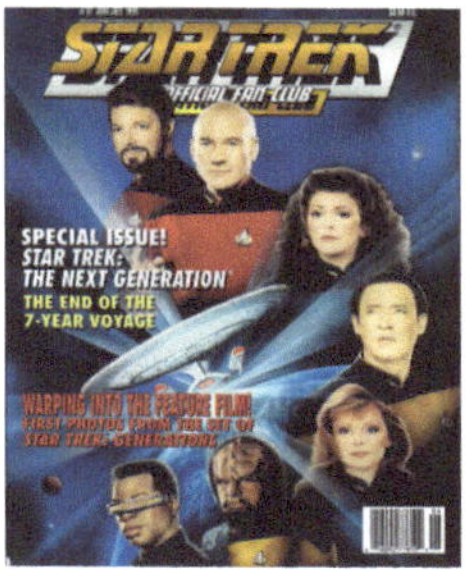

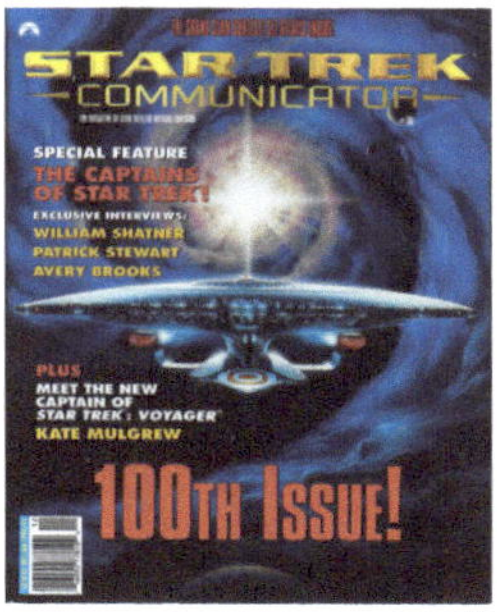

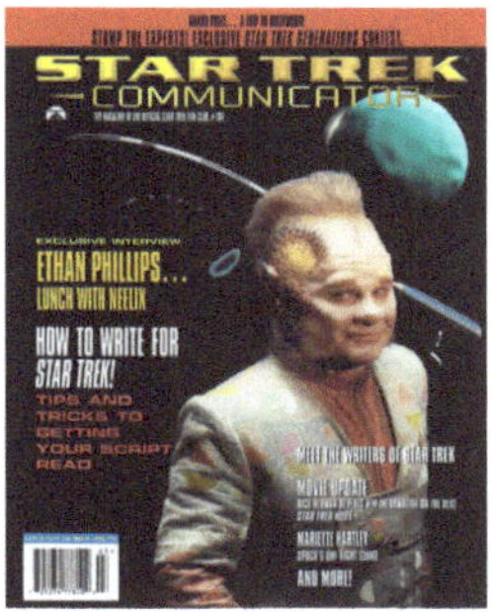

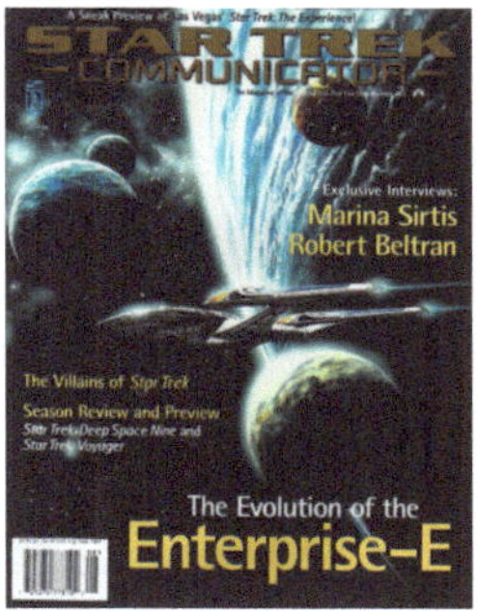

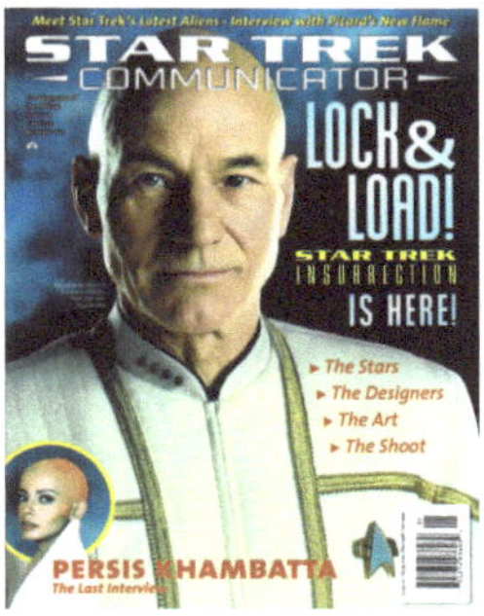

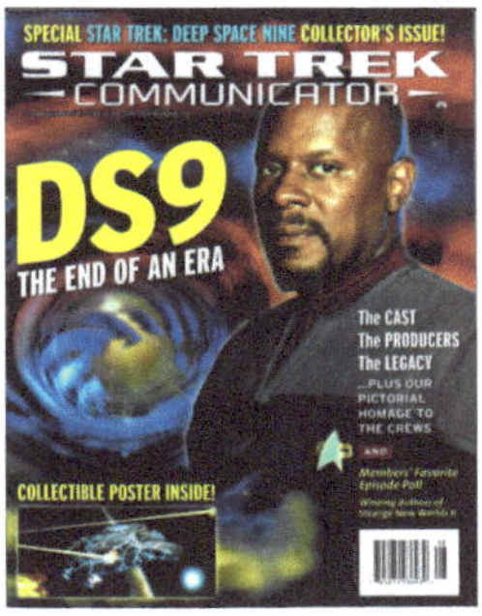

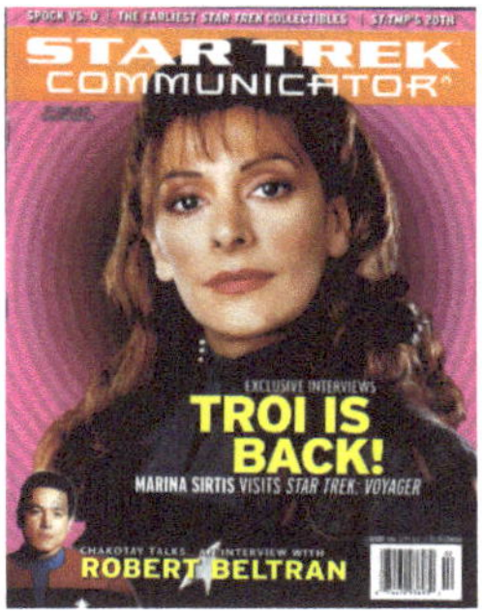

READ ABOUT SALMAN'S ADVENTURES IN FOOD, TRAVEL, AND HIS INTERVIEWS WITH BARKER, BROOKS, AND TAKEI

"Very engaging writing style, Sal—just like when you tell stories verbally. This is your strongest suit. . . . McDermid was right—you're a good writer, and I agree that you could sell this shit to a big house with all the stories you have. No doubt of it."

BRETT SAVORY
Author (Hobb's Editions)

On the following pages are a few examples of my writing.
I do hope you enjoy.

Travel

Food

Interviews

"Very engaging writing style, Sal—just like when you tell stories verbally. This is your strongest suit. . . . McDermid was right—you're a good writer, and I agree that you could sell this shit to a big house with all the stories you have. No doubt of it."

BRETT SAVORY
Author (Hobb's Editions)

HOW TO STEAL A RICKSHAW (BANGLADESH)

by Salman A. Nensi

Subject: Wanna buy a rickshaw?

A hooker, three thousand takka and a rickshaw...

...or, just another typical night's adventure with Azim and Sal...

Tonight I took Azim out to a Korean restaurant for dinner. Strange to eat Korean food in the middle of Dhakka but there are, apparently, quite a number of Koreans living and working here and yes, just like all the Indians and Pakistanis living in Bangladesh, they're in the import/export garment business. (Please do not forget to move your head from side to side as you say "import/export" in your best Indian accent!) I did manage to freak out a Korean the other day when I went for a walk in the sauna-like heat by saying hello in Korean. He wasn't sure I'd said it,and when he realized there wasn't anyone else who could have, he just looked confused and hurried along his way. <> I love doing that! Hee hee...

Bangladesh is a dry country... no booze allowed and I wanted to get a bottle of that insane Korean rice wine soju for Azim to get a true taste of

Korea and so I went to sweet-talk the owner. I managed to convince her let us have what she said was her husband's last bottle of soju by telling her how much I missed Seoul and how happy I was to find a Korean restaurant in Dhakka (she's promised to make me some dok buk ghee next visit as it's not on the menu and I told her how much I missed my adjumas!) <> So after a semi-decent meal (The kim chee was sub-par, at best —which the owner knew and came over to apologize for; the salmon sushi was so off it scared us and the service, well, that's a just a whole rant in and of itself!) Azim and I went on an adventure to find some shang.

His driver drops us off at the apartment building (a small five-story building, with very large four-bedroom apartments appointed fully in three-tone marble) and we hop into the other car and drive off looking for the ABC Tower. Yesterday, at the International Club, Azim asked the "Jim Belushi of Dhakka" where one might score something to smoke and he directed us to find the ABC Tower and the dark alleyway next to it. So that's what we were looking for, some dark alleyway near the ABC Tower...

We find a likely looking alleyway, park the car and turn off the lights. Sure enough someone approaches us, just as Dhakka Jim said they would, and offers us something. My heart leaps in joy and anticipation of a nice smoke... but it isn't someone selling hash, it's some young Bangladeshi woman in a sari offering us her services. Now, I've seen hookers in all sorts of countries all over the world but for some reason a hooker in a sari just seems very very wrong to me. Nonetheless we're on a mission and so we ask her if she knows where we can get something to smoke. She of course points us to the cigarette sellers who line the intersections here at all hours of the day and night.... No no no, we want something to *smoke* we say again in English... assuming she'll get it the second time. Azim is saying "smoke, smoke" while I do my mime of sucking on a dube but nope, the lady is none the wiser. She decides we must be drunk or want to get drunk and tries to get us to join her somewhere nearby for some drinks, doing her own mime of drunkards up-ending a bottle down their throats. We're not getting through to her and Azim, being Azim, begins to mock saying in a sing song voice, "Bob Marley! Ganja! Smoke!!" and that, yep, that she understood, no problem. Hashish? What the hell is that, but ganja, the Jamaican word, yeah that she gets no problem! Hee hee... but even so, no, she can't help us so we drive the car around the block again, find the ABC Tower and look for a different dark alleyway.

Now why can't they be civilized and put up some signage to help us poor expat/tourist types... this alleyway for hookers, this one for hash, this one for pirated DVDs and books... that would be a good idea since all these items are supposed to be in ready supply here and sooner or later all expats succumb to their desires for entertainment... or so I've been told!

For the next half hour, Azim and I end up driving around various dark alleyways, talking to taxi drivers; lost Saudi tourists; some young street urchins; a couple of security guards / night watchmen and various other flotsam and jetsam of the night. We give up. No one has a clue where to find what we're looking for but at least now we know the Bengali word for shang... it's ganja, not hasish!

As we turn the car to leave one of the security guards, who is supposed to be guarding the building we found him in front of, chases us down the street to tell us that in fact he has found something. Again that telltale leap in my heart... But what he had found was a rickshaw walla who said he could take us to find some shang—not as good as finding shang, but at least we're getting closer! He wants to get into our car but we figure it's safer to follow his rickshaw instead and so we do... at like, 5km/h as he pedals his vehicle and we follow faithfully behind him, making sure we don't lose him in the sea of rickshaws that cover the Dhakka streets. We follow him to the Gulshan 2 Circle (a main intersection near where we live) and pull over to the side, parking where he waves for us to stop.

Negotiating a price for shang is always interesting, in whatever country I happen to be in. Out in this part of the world shang is rather cheap, however, as a tourist one always gets ripped off. We don't pay the local price for the stuff... ever! But even so, being ripped off still means we're usually paying less here than we do at home... or if we're not, we're so happy to be able to have some shang we don't care that it's costing us more than it should. So Mr. Rickshaw Walla and I start talking and he starts at 4,000 taka for 50 grams and we settle on a price of 3,000. Azim says we should keep going to 2,500 but I'm feeling the need and just want to get this guy on his way so we can go home and have a smoke. I hand him six crisp new 500 taka notes and he smiles.... A good sign I think... idiot!

For those of you are currency curious, 70 taka makes a Canadian dollar so 3,000 taka is about $42. And with 50 grams, that makes about 100 small regular paper size dubes, which works out to about 50¢ a joint. Not a bad price—not a great one either, but not bad. Mr. Walla gives the security guard / night watchman, who is guarding the building we've parked in front of, 10 taka to watch his rickshaw while he goes off to get us some shang. He tells us that he is leaving his rickshaw as security (that's our story and we're sticking to it!) and that he'll be back in 20 minutes. We smile, sit back and relax with the full knowledge and happiness that always comes with an impending shang delivery.

One hour later, though, we're still waiting...

At this point we're tired, it's 1:00 a.m. and our initial excitement of having scored a stash has degenerated into disappointment at being ripped off. We figure, however, that the rickshaw must now rightfully belong to us and Azim and I begin silly talk of taking it home and perhaps putting it into one of the walls of a house like that car in the City TV building in Toronto that has the wheels still moving. And as we keep talking we figure, yeah, why not... we should take the rickshaw and so we begin negotiations with the night watchman on how to get the thing back to Azim's place.

Since we're at a major intersection there are a group of kids selling cigarettes and we figure one of them can pedal the rickshaw back to Azim's place for a few taka, but getting the night watchman to understand what we want to do is not easy... and now suddenly we're surrounded by four of five of the cigarette children all trying to help this man understand what we want to do while they make fun of him as he's apparently deaf! The negotiations centre around who exactly is going to pedal the damned thing to our place and how is that person going to get back here and what will we pay and where is Mr. Walla and through all of this the night watchman does not look pleased... of course, he has been charged to wait and watch the rickshaw and he's been paid to do so...

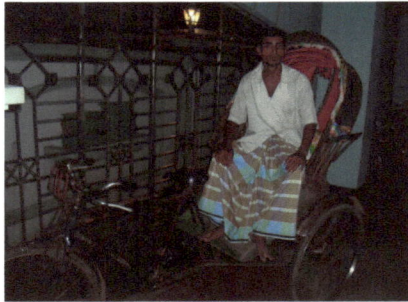

Azim and I speak Gujerati, not Hindi or Bengali and so the negotiations are a combination of hand guestures; the 30% of words our languages have in common and everyone else's broken English. It takes 10 people, all with various grasps of the English language, to help negotiate, but finally we're done... for 100 taka, less than a buck fifty, Abdul will take me and the rickshaw to Azim's place while his friend will ride his own rickshaw behind us so that he can go about his business when he's done dealing with these two daft foreigners. This is good news for me 'cause for a few moments there it looked like I was going to have to drive the thing back myself and while that would have been fine exercise the idea did not, as you can imagine, thrill me overly. But now Mr. Night Watchman is not happy... he has an obligation and everyone around him seems to have forgotten that. He voices his concern which of course is stifled when I hand him 10 taka... he grins and yes, he will tell Mr. Walla where his rickshaw is, if and when he ever returns.

So there I am at 2:00 a.m., in a rickshaw being driven by Abdul, followed in a rickshaw being driven by one of Abdul's friends, and Azim in the car following two rickshaws at about 5 km/h down the main road! At some point along the way to the apartment, a white car pulls up alongside my rickshaw. Abdul has a conversation with the driver and tells the driver but that I paid it 2000 taka to Mr. Walla for some hashish but the rest of the conversation was lost on me. I told Abdul I'd paid 2000 just in case he was going to offer to get me some... no point in him knowing I'd paid Mr. Walla too much, eh! Anyway, the guy in the car, and where the hell he came from, I have no idea. But the guy nods and then drives off, leaving us to go along our merry way...

Adbul is now telling me that Mr. Walla is not a very good businessman and that night time it is not a good time to be roaming around Dhakka trying to score some hash... well, that much we could have told him ourselves! Abdul, however, is a VERY good businessman and has a cell phone (half the country is starving and can't afford to eat and yet the guy pedaling the rickshaw for a living in the torn shirt, ratty shorts and sandals, yes him, he has a cell phone! Weird world...) Abdul admonishes me for not getting him to help him out instead of the untrustworthy Mr. Walla. "You can be calling to me anytime, Sir... anytime, 8 o'clock, 9 o'clock, 10 o'clock in the morning... anytime Sir and I am bringing to you what you are to be needing, yes Sir..." Well then... I mean why didn't he just say that earlier! "Yes Sir, if you are needing the hashisha or the mar-u-anna or the brown sugar, no problem... I am to be delivering it to you. You are a good business man Sir, you have a cell phone, I have a cell phone, you are calling, I am bringing..." yep, I get you... no worries, except I'm just a lousy Canadian tourist with no cell phone but don't worry, Saheib in the car has one! <>

Azim now pulls alongside so we can discuss that weirdness with the white car and laugh about the fact that we've kinda absconded with a rickshaw and are blocking the entire road as we laze along at the speed of Abdul's feet... Abdul is enjoying himself... we are all "good businessmen" and this has thrilled him. Then goes on to tell me that he far prefers mar-u-anna to the hashisha and when I agree with him, that I do too, I'm treated to an even bigger smile. Oh yes, good businessmen, one and all! But what the hell is "brown sugar?"

Upon getting to Azim's apartment we now have to explain to his guards why he's in the car, I'm on a rickshaw and no, actually the rickshaw IS coming into the parking lot and well maybe someone will come to claim it, or maybe they won't... we're not sure... but you know, if someone does show up, just call us and we'll come down and sort it out... oh and no, don't tell him which apartment we're in, just call us! Yes, Mr. Walla has our money, yes he took it and will bring it back or we get to keep his rickshaw... dubious looks abound but well Azim is Mr. Azim to you so, put the damned rickshaw to one side and call us if Mr. Walla shows up, cool? Cool.

I end up giving Abdul 200 taka 'cause he's a better businessman than I am and he's making me feel guilty and stupid and making me promise to call him in the morning because hash business is best done in the morning and not at 2:00 a.m.... I promise Azim will call and give him the extra 100 taka. Grinning, he drives off with his friend and Azim and I stand for a moment, as the guards lock the gates, and stare at our new possession... it's a zany contraption on three wheels, with a small uncomfortable park bench type seat, a hard plastic seat for the driver, who always stands and pedals anyway, and a broken retracting canopy in case the monsoon hits and you're out in the middle of it... like that would do any good as the rain here falls in blankets, not just sheets! The back is all decked out in colourful stickers and images from myths and movies or something and, unlike the other rickshaws, this one has a blank space on the back, in the middle of which is the sign for infinity... vague notions of Douglas Adams float around in our heads as we head up the stairs to the elevator.

That was about three hours ago. It is now 5:00 a.m. Mr. Walla hasn't shown up yet and so I am beginning to think that we really have just purchased a rather interesting souvenir of Bangladesh for fifty bucks! A good thing Azim's company gives him a shipping allowance when his contract ends... or maybe I've found my new business idea... Salman, Rickshaw Walla? Azim was still laughing as he went to bed I am still chuckling as I type this... The world is a funny place when you're a shang head!

Lets see what tomorrow brings... as long as it's not the cops yelling at us for stealing a rickshaw, it'll be all good...

NENSI.COM

Ten Days in Kabul

Adventures with Omar, Oliver, Ahmed, Sal, a pointy camera and a big yellow taxi!

written by Salman A. Nensi, photography by Oliver Strong

"Hello, I just want to say that if something unfortunate has befallen me that Salman is in no way responsible. I went to Afghanistan of my own free will, knowing the risks. Lots of love to all."

Oliver

Ten Days in Kabul

Adventures with Omar, Oliver, Ahmed, Sal, a pointy camera and a big yellow taxi!

"Hello, I just want to say that if something unfortunate has befallen me that Salman is in no way responsible. I went to Afghanistan of my own free will, knowing the risks. Lots of love to all." —Oliver

Well I had to get him to write something, didn't I? We were heading to Afghanistan, not Palm Beach, to a country where there were over 2,000 civilian deaths in 2008. The UN estimates that 60 percent of the Afghan population has been directly affected by the war and that a staggering 96% of Afghans have been negatively affected in some way. Kidnappings are routine—they can ask for as little as $1,500 for your return which doesn't sound like much until you realize that the "official" minimum wage is US $42 a month, and hardly anyone gets the official amount, most get far, far less. So it's totally possible that the guy sitting next to you at the restaurant could be either ready to kidnap you or instead harbouring a nice little explosive device under his kurta along with a yen for those seventy-two virgins awaiting his triumphant arrival in the afterlife. The way of life is very different over here and it's important to remember that.

I should, for those of you who don't know him, describe Oliver, my travel companion. He's tall...white...blond...and did I mention white? And blond? All I could hear in my head is my English godmother saying,

"Doesn't he stick out a bit like a sore thumb, luv?" And yeah, surrounded by us darker-skinned, darker-haired lads, Oliver does stick out. It's the hair, really, although there are some blue-eyed, fair Afghans, as well those with red hair and eyes of all shapes and colours. As a result of the history of the place and its geographic location, many would-be conquerors have left bits of their armies and DNA here in this land, and their traits can still be seen in certain individuals and peoples. Humans have been living in Afghanistan for over 50,000 years by some estimates—making this one of the first places humans farmed and had permanent settlements. The territory has been far larger than what we currently call Afghanistan and was conquered by both the Median and Persian empires in their time. Alexander the Great passed through as did the Seleucids, the Indo-Greeks, the Indians, the Turks and the Mongols. In more modern times the Brits, the Russians and now the Americans, aka International Security Force, are all trying to control and subdue the place and the peoples. Soldiers do what soldiers do, and here it has been no different. Afghanistan is a geneticist's dream.

Back to Oliver. Mr. Oliver Kenneth Luke Strong, as well as being white and blond, is also very cute, fit, young and funny. He cooks well, reads books, is a soccer goalie and a brilliant photographer and single. Interested female readers may get in touch with me about him, though you'll be competing for his favours with Naim's father—Naim being a fellow we met at the house of our Afghan driver—but I'm getting ahead of the story.

So the plan was to drive to Kabul from Dushanbe, Tajikistan where we we'd been hanging out with friends for a few weeks. The drive was easy enough—I'd done the part from Dushanbe to the boarder on my last trip. Would take half a day and then apparently 6-8 hours from the border down to Kabul with maybe a small side trip to Mazar, a neat city in the North with great architecture and tonnes of OLD...I like old. Old roads, buildings, paths, gardens, etc...Afghanistan's got a goodly amount of old.

I wanted to go back to Kabul, in part because I wanted to scout out work for my company (which specializes in preparing complex reports for UN agencies and the like) and in part because we'd been invited to the wedding of Omar, an Afghan friend. Omar was going to drive up to the border and meet us with his uncle the "commander." I never did find out what he was the commander of—we met a lot of "commanders" on this part of our journey and figured sometimes it's best not to be too inquisitive.

But as our departure date loomed closer, we kept getting more and more advice NOT to drive down. The security situation was deteriorating as we watched. The number of bombings was up. Some organizations never targeted before were now being hit. Kidnappings were on the rise, the asking figure for getting people back had dropped. The last time I was here you had to BE someone to get kidnapped. Now you just had to look like you had access to a grand. Eventually Omar's mum told him she'd rather he not drive up to the border to meet the foreigners, and my mum was asking why I wanted to do this part of the trip in the first place. Mums are like that. They worry.

The question of why comes up a lot. My usual answer is a flippant, "Why not?" or a "'Cause it's there!" but I know those aren't really satisfactory responses to others as they come off as flippant. Maybe the best answer I can think of comes from a book, *Shadow of the Silk Road* by

Colin Thubron, who ponders the same question and says, "A hundred reasons clamour for your going," and after listing some, he concludes, "You go to see what will happen."

And that's it really. I go to see what will happen. What will happen to me, to friends, to places; what will happen with food, with drinks, with smokeables; what will happen to me after drinks and smokeables. Maybe it's that in all the various places I call home, I know what will happen, and so I need to go places where for once I don't know.

Omar has been patiently waiting at the airport for us for a few hours. Even with the flight delay and our delay with forms, he's smiling his wide, gorgeous smile and is very pleased to see us. I'm pleased to see him again too. We worked together at the Serena Hotel the last time I was in Kabul and became friends. We've kept in touch over the years by email but I hadn't seen him in a while. He's heavier than when I last saw him, which becomes rather the topic for our time in Kabul—what to do to lose weight before the wedding.

Walking out of the airport, we see guys with guns everywhere. At gates, in cars, just chillin' by a tree. It's weird and surreal...and not at all comforting in the way those who like guns suggest it should be. Really, being surrounded by guys with guns, even if they are on my side (and I hope they are) is just not as comforting as being in a place where no one has guns! It boggles my mind that this simple idea, this is such a hard thing to grasp? Yo, Heston—you listening?

We get to the taxi we've hired for the week. Ahmed is our driver and we quickly christen him Mario Andretti. He's like a daemon in the car and I'm both very pleased by this and scared shitless. Speed means we can get away fast if we need to. Speed also means higher risk of crashing into some other git, also speeding around! There was talk of hiring a proper 4x4 large white SUV like so many of the foreigners and diplomatic corps have here and in other third world places. We discount this for several reasons:

- The taxi is yellow and can easily blend in with the other yellow cabs. Yes, just like NYC, it's all yellow cabs here. (Of course these taxis are older than I am and they look like papier-mâché because the metal's so crumpled, with all the bends and scratches and accidents banged out of the chassis over and over and over again. Nothing here is terribly roadworthy in a Western sense, but then the roads are not terribly roadworthy in a Western sense either so it's all good.)

- Large white cars are a bit easier to hit with rockets than a small yellow cab going fast.
- The cost of a large car, driver and our own guy with a gun is just silly.
- Ahmed, our driver, is well experienced, having driven taxi in Kabul for years and also having spent a few years driving in Tehran. The man can drive.

Ahmed's smile is wide and broad with a few teeth missing. His face is warm and friendly, suggesting that he's happy and content. Hair akimbo under his traditional hat, his face is a bit weather-worn but he's got a great handshake. So, feeling good about our choice of transportation, we head to our guest house. There are still very few or no trees on roads. The drought continues mercilessly, nothing is growing and a layer of fine, grey-brown soot the consistency of dust has fallen on everything. You get the impression that if you stopped outside to smoke a cigarette you too would come back inside with a layer of dust on you. I did and I did.

The guest house is a large old family dwelling that is walled. The place is tatty— rugs, wallpaper, paintings, sheets, carpets, all faded and threadbare. It's as if you were staying at your grandmother's place that might have had grandeur fifty years before she was born but is now just a pale and ghostly remnant. We are two of about ten guests, most of whom seem to be Indians and Pakistanis. They're here working because no one else will. Many of them work for Japanese engineering firms and travel all over the country—Japanese engineers won't come and work in Afghanistan. The first time I sat down at dinner with the other guests, I grabbed some bread and chillies and munched while others grabbed the rice and curries. Several of the guys were looking at me

a bit askance but then approval crosses their faces. Even if I was born in the West and have a funny accent, I'm still one of them at heart! Chillies save me again.

Chillies and bread…that's all I need. I have the same non verbal communication with all the guys working at the guest house, "No, nothing for lunch, but please leave two loaves of bread and some fresh chillies in my room, thank you. Breakfast? Ah, no thanks…but if you have some chillies and some bread I'll munch that in the car." They think I'm nuts. I know I am. But being nuts over chillies is cool here.

I have to take a moment and rapture about the bread in Central Asia. It is phenomenal. I'm not sure what it is. Maybe it's the clay ovens it's baked in? The onion seeds sprinkled on top? The water in the region? The unbleached, unprocessed flour, butter and salt? All I know is I put on a lot of weight on this trip—all due to the bread in Dushanbe and Kabul.

The staff at the guest house are all male except for, surprisingly to me, one older woman. She might have been the mother of one of the workers, not sure...she looked old enough to have children in their thirties. She'd show up in the morning after the Indians had all gone to work and I was never sure what she did besides give me lovely smiles and do a little ironing. Not that one should underestimate the skill it takes to iron here. The iron is an ancient lump of metal, like a mini anvil with a handle welded to it. There is a cord for the power but it's all frayed and looks like the iron might explode if you plug it in and left it alone. Mind you, the power here is only on for *some* time (sometimes a long time, sometimes a short time—you know, on for *some* time), then you have to switch to a generator. So the whole house has two sets of plugs, one for regular power and one for the generator power, and every time the regular power goes off, you re-plug everything over to the other set of sockets. Everything has to be switched—refrigerator, water cooler, Internet routers, etc. Oh, and FYI, there's no ironing board, it's a piece of wood on the floor covered by a towel. How people here can iron shirts properly without that curvy bit on the end of an ironing board I'm not sure. But they do.

Ahmed is waiting in the car, Omar has come inside to get us. Before we go out we check through the peephole in the door. Yep, Ahmed is there, his awesome grin lighting up his face. Across the small street I can see the two guards who operate the single pole barrier and a few of the other guard houses down the road. It all looks calm and safe. Like I would know what to look for anyway, but I'm somehow in the lead again and so it looks good and we go. (You people really trust me to know if we should open the front door or not? You're all balmy!)

Open the door. Go. No dawdling. No waiting. No lingering goodbyes. Around here you MOVE! Kabul is not a place you hang out outside, especially in areas full of foreign types. Your shoes, coat, bag are all ready. You check the door and head straight to your assigned seat in the car. You get in fast and shut the door, locking it right away. All three of us are in and we're moving again—fast. The barrier guys have opened the gate and we pull into traffic. It's like a segment from a ballet that, with a bit of practice, soon becomes one coordinated, smooth manoeuvre for us. Every time we get into the car, get out of the car, head somewhere—it's the same ballet piece.

A few moments later you hear five gun shots and you know you will never see your relatives again.

Our first stop of the day is to see one of my Beyond Reports new staffers. Maryam is an interesting lady. Most of the senior male members of her family are gone. Dead in various wars, skirmishes and terrorist acts that have plague Kabul for decades. It is always surreally funny to me that in the West we make such a big deal about terrorist attacks and security, etc. when in places like this "terror" is just a fact of life. In places like Kabul it's actually not so terror-inducing to be there, it just is. I suspect it was like this in London in the '70s while the IRA was going nuts. It was common to hear a bomb blast a few streets over and then read about the damage in the evening paper. It didn't seem to be all that terrifying because, after a while, humans get used to anything that's around them. Admittedly I was a child back then in the UK so of course I wasn't terrified of anything. For one thing I had my brother, Grieg, on my side. He could and did take care of pretty much all that ailed me as a kid.

Terror for the Afghans happens in ways we in the West just simply can not comprehend. Try this one: Karim, 24, cook. We meet, become friends and one day, on the top of a mountain overlooking Kabul where we sit with his friends he asks me, "So, tell me true...do they all think we are terrorists?" And by "they" he means us...us Western types who have money and arms and control over the world... do we all think all Afghans are terrorists. It breaks my heart. I think about it for a bit and have to say yes, the answer is yes...in my view a vast majority of those living in the West would look at Karim and his group of friends—all

20-something lads who know how to use guns and have ALL killed at least one human—and see them as terrorists.

Imagine you are at home. With your wife, children and perhaps brother with his kids. You live in a nice neighbourhood, suburban with trees and kids playing in parks... you know the type of place, Western looking, peaceful. There is a knock at the door. You open it and there are 5 guys with guns at the door. They wish for all the male members of the family over 12 to come with them. What do you do? Well. You go...they've got guns and your children are targets. Now you are sixty members of your family in one jail cell. It is a box with bars. No toilet, no running water, just one very small and insufficient bucket in the corner for defecating into. Each morning they show up and take five of you out of the cell. A few moments later you hear five gun shots and you know you will never see your relatives again.

Out of sixty male members of his family, fewer than a dozen survived the Taliban's visit to his town. He survived as he can cook. His cousin can cut hair, he also survived. Someone explain this to me. If I hate you enough to kill all your family, how do I then internally rationalize keeping you as a my cook or haircutter? Is that a bit daft? Or am I the only one who thinks so?

So back to Maryam. Because most of her family is gone, she's taken over providing and caring for those that are left. She's a bank manager and responsible for a large branch of tellers and staff. We arrive in the morning and are served hot, milky tea and coffee and a gorgeous deep glass plate with raised dividers sectioning off different fruits and nuts—and really tasty and delicious stuff too! Every house, every meeting, everywhere, it's all about the super-sweet tea and coffee and the fruit and nut plates. Made a nice change from the weird Soviet type candies we were served when visiting friends in Tajikistan.

Maryam's smart, funny, personable and capable. Most of her work really takes place in the late afternoon after the tellers are closed up and she has to do the reconciliations, etc. We've given her a cell phone that can access the Net and during the day she's making calls for us trying to sell the various services Beyond Reports offers. I can't imagine her staying at home, making curry and waiting for her man to come home with orders and demands. She is what I think of when I read stories about Kabul in the '70s—full of smart, progressive women in all aspects of life.

As we leave the bank, it is brighter, the sun is climbing but the town still looks grey. We're at a strip mall somewhere in a 'burb and the parking lot and structure look just like they would in any American or Canadian town.

Except that there are barriers on the parking lot entrance and several guys with AK 47s floating around protecting us and our car. I worry about two foreign guys emerging from a bank. Don't they just scream "target" and "money?" I think too much. It's not that bad

the car and he seems to be a part of the restaurant we've just parked in front of so that's a comfort. In Kabul, as in other places I've been, kids of all ages are everywhere doing all sorts of little gigs for a pittance here and a pittance there. I understand child labour laws

here. We'll be fine. Maybe we should run anyway? Ahmed is dutifully waiting for us, as he always is, and we jump in the yellow taxi and are off again—destination lunch!

We pull up by the side of another busy road—three lanes of traffic each direction with a wide avenue-style median which was, I'm sure, lined with trees at some point but is now just a garbage and dust collection point. We park the car, leaving our belongings inside, including Oliver's bag with his cost-more-than-you'll-make-in-a-year-or-possibly-two laptop. I'm not so sure that's wise but we've paid a kid 10Afg (21 cents US) to watch

but these kids have a simple choice: work or starve to death...what good are child labour laws in places like this?

The entryway is small and there are kebabs being grilled out front in massive quantities. Spindly metal legs hold up at least four metal trough of four feet by half a foot, full of red hot coals constantly being fanned by a man we'll call the Kebab Guy. Atop the trough are laid skewer after skewer of gorgeous-smelling meat. Kebab Guy turns them, spices them, fans the coals and it's like a factory. Waiters come to collect the done skewers while kitchen staff bring out fresh ones for roasting. This

place does over 200 kilograms of mutton every lunch time, every day of the week, every day of the year. We enter the place and it's full of locals sitting on low raised platforms that are covered in carpets eating around low tables, quintessential Asian style, with piles of bread and mounds of kebabs. Apparently it's one of the most famous kebab houses in all of Kabul, and Omar figures since no foreigner has ever come here (and the restaurant staff confirmed this) we're safe. I'm not so sure about his logic but how does one turn down a meal in a famous Kabul kebab house? Simple. You don't.

The restaurant keeps going and going. It's obviously taken over the store next door and the house behind it and the one behind that and, just for good measure, the one over there too. We keep walking farther and farther inside and I'm getting more and more concerned. There is absolutely no getting out of here fast if we needed to and we've walked past hundreds of local guys any of whom could have Talib sympathies or simply see us as a good way of getting a few thousand by holding us for ransom. Each face is a potential threat as well as a potential friend. How to tell the difference? Am I any good at reading people, faces, body language? Nope!

Putting aside the fear and trepidation, we keep following Omar and eventually end up at the back of the place in the far corner and finally get to sit. My back is to the wall… my back is almost ALWAYS to the wall and I realize that I'll get to see them coming for me and there's nowhere for me to go, except through the wall.

Ahmed takes a small three-foot-by-two carpet off one wall—many prayer carpets for customers to use line the wall —and goes to the other side of the room to pray; Omar and I are bad, we're not into that so much. We are, however, both into kebabs and soon enough we are all deep in a glorious heap of deliciousness.

Ahmed rejoins us and wastes no time digging in. And it keeps coming. Waiters roam the dark passageways with several fans of six skewers each, laying them artfully down on the naan being used as a plate. You get a tray, it's layered with bread and then with the barbequed lamb. The meat is still hot and still frying, so the drip-

ping fat makes the bread mouth-wateringly ready for eating too. Extra salt, pepper and chilli powder are available for sprinkling onto the skewers and we eat and eat and eat. Omar orders more kebabs and we think this is way to much food but again it all disappears.

Omar's weight comes up again, and we try telling him to go easy on the bread but he's a Kabuli and that's like telling a Korean to go easy on the rice—just not going to happen. The chef has come to the back to see us eating, and a few more of the locals have stopped eating to watch us. An older man, eighty or more, I'm sure, tells Omar it is good that he brings us here, so that we can see how Afghans eat and that sharing bread and food with foreigners is a good thing. Omar tells the old man we are friends from years ago and have kept in touch. The old man's eyes crinkle with smiles and warmth—he clearly approves of our friendship.

Well fed again, we pile into the car; all the belongings are still there and the kid asks for a bit more money as he had to take care of the car with the foreigners' stuff in it. Ahmed gives him a telling off about treating foreigners properly and pays him the standard amount and, zanily as always, we pull into the flow of what constitutes Kabul traffic—kind of like you'd imagine —no rules, everyone jockeying for position, speeding along with strange looking contraptions that have motors on them, cars and trucks and busses that look like they were made a hundred years ago and then put through a dishwasher and of course the occasional donkey and cart. Surreal. Over and over again this place is just surreal.

Later we pull up to a very large brown wall—The Babur Gardens.

A few years ago I was here when the Gardens were being restored. The same man who had overseen the restoration of the massive park in Cairo's city centre was brought over to work on this site, which is over five hundred years old. Back then Kabul was so lush, so green, so fertile, so beautiful, that Muhammad Zahir al-Din Babur, founder of the Mogul dynasty (1526-1857), determined to be laid to rest here. So he created this garden—

87 - Writing

his favourite of ten he had constructed around Kabul during his reign.

Reading ancient accounts of the gardens one is awed; travelers of the time never failed to be impressed by their scale and beauty. They included a huge gateway with golden cupolas; several pools; marble channels through which water cascaded down twelve terraces; large, lush trees providing shade in the hot summer months; and the magnificent mausoleum that houses Babur's remains and which survives today. But what was once an eleven-hectare garden of avenues that spanned the western slope of Kabul has been reborn as a modest park for locals well within the city itself. It's nice enough—until one thinks back to what it was.

To restore it, local Afghanis had to be re-taught carpentry and stone masonry. Those overseeing the work had to import marble and craftspeople from the Middle East and India and Pakistan, because there was no one left in Kabul who could have made what Kabul was once famed for. Artisans, craftspeople, stone-workers...all are gone, long dead in one war or another and dead long before they could

pass on their knowledge to anyone else. Who cared how to carve marble? People wanted to learn how to take apart their AK 47s. So now they do, and the glory of Kabul will never be again—unless the Aga Khan Trust for Culture AKTC (a Muslim philanthropic organization with strong connections to Canada) has a say in it, and luckily it does.

Babur still lies in the brilliant white, hand-carved marble mausoleum, atop the final terrace of the garden. Garden? Sigh. It is all dust and grey and a shallow shudder of what once was. An earthquake in 1842 and the myriad subsequent conflicts have taken their toll on the site. The trees have been cut down for firewood and the majority of the walls have been destroyed by years of neglect and fighting or have otherwise been carried away, piece by piece, to be used as building materials for newer constructions. And the years of drought have done little to help.

The rebuilding of the garden is just one of many projects being spearheaded here by the AKTC. The idea is to make a place where the residents will want to live with respect for their own culture and their own history. The Aga Khan believes development should be multipronged: you should give people not only ways to learn again and grow food again but also ways to take pride again in who they are, where they are and what they have accomplished and can accomplish. Sounds like a nice idea. I wonder if it's working?

Unfortunately for us it will take a long time before this garden will be anything resembling "magnificent" again. Currently the almond trees look as if they will not be producing anything besides sad yellow leaves until sometime next century. Lights have been set up to make the garden a lovely place to visit in the evening, but there is no electricity. There is a wa-

ter channel, but no water flows in it. Oliver has the sense that one day things will turn around, but I'm more pessimistic. Up near the mausoleum is a pool of water—or what should have been a pool of sparkling, fresh, clean water. It is now a low, sunken pool of green gunk full of plastic bottles, potato-crisp bags, cookie and candy wrappers, pop cans, cigarette butts…I could go on. Someone explain this to me. Why does any fenced-off area or any body of water encourage humans to dump their trash in it? Is it a sign that Kabul is getting wealthier again? If a country is really poor, nothing is thrown out, it is all reused until it really has no life left in it and then it is recycled. The garbage was sad, disappointing and typical. Humans really are pathetic…capable of such magnificence but all too often the base nature of just not giving a rat's ass comes to the fore.

The mausoleum, at least, is beautiful, its marble work intricate and breathtaking. Carvings of Arabic script flow over the tomb, caressing and swaddling it like a comforter of vines. The walls surrounding the tomb are all carved in a design of lattice work, through which you can see the outside world. It is cold, the marble. This place is a bit cold too. I keep trying to picture Kabul as a garden the way it's described in history books, but it's not so easy when everything around you is blanketed in dust, and the distant sound of car horns ensures you know you're in the 21st century. Up here we're a bit away from the traffic so there is a smidgen of peace. I've been resting my hand on the marble trying to feel something—a connection to the past, maybe…? But I feel nothing. There is no mystery left here for me. I can sense no power, no connectivity. I only come off as a hippy when not with my hippy

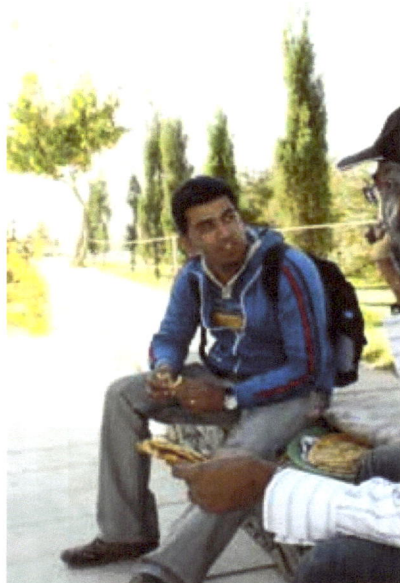

friends and I don't often search for the "energy" of a place, but from time to time I feel it and find it. I was hoping the same would be true here, but there is nothing for me.

I looked up the translation of the inscription after getting back to the guest house: "Only this mosque of beauty, this temple of nobility, constructed for the prayer of saints and the epiphany of cherubs, was fit to stand in so venerable a sanctuary as this highway of archangels, this theatre of heaven, the light garden of the god-forgiven angel king whose rest is in the garden of heaven, Zahiruddin Muhammad Babur the Conqueror." Might be a bit much for my tombstone but it's got a ring to it.

Over the walls to the west, the hills continue to rise up and are covered with dwellings almost to the top. All the hills that surround the city are home to people. Poor people of course, as on the hills there is no plumbing and are no power lines. In the courtyard of one of the walled compounds on the hill we can see people in colourful outfits—there's a wedding going on—but it's too far up too make out much more than people in colourful clothes. Oliver wants to take pictures and I think he snaps off a few before Omar warns that there might be trouble if someone thinks we're taking photos of their women.

I was admonished for the same type of thing in the car at some point. I was in the back seat and we were stuck in traffic. There were two adorable kids in the car next to us and they of course could see that I was a foreigner. I smiled and waved at them. They smiled and waved back. Omar told me off. There were women in the car and I needed to be more careful or the husband would assume I was trying to contact his women and this would be enough for him to cause trouble. What type of "trouble" I figured I didn't need to know. I mean, it's Kabul, everyone has a bloody AK47…is there any other type of trouble around these parts?

Ahmed and I walked slowly around the gardens together communicating without using words. My fault, not his: he speaks a number of languages, none of which I speak. Ahmed speaks Farsi, Dari, Pashto, Turkish and something else I can't remember. We communicated pretty well though. I'm getting quite good at these non-verbal, non-English ways of talking. Being a bit of a ham and being good at charades helps. Context helps too. If you're in a restaurant, it's easier for the non-English-speaking person to assume you want food and drink. And a surprising number of words in Dari and Farsi are similar to words in Gujarati, the other language I claim to be able to speak well aside from English—my godmother will tell you I speak dreadfully ever since I moved to the "colonies," i.e., Canada!

So…what should we do next with our sightseeing day? Well I already know what I want to do next and Ahmed is in agreement (context and miming and we are now FAST friends) and since he's the driver we're off to his place for a sheesha and smoke with some friends. Some friends? Hmmmm. Okay, is this a good idea? We don't know Ahmed very well, nor do we know any of his friends. Who are these people? I haven't even had a smoke and already it feels like my buzz has been killed by my over-thinking the security again.

Omar may be sensing I'm a little apprehensive and goes on a bit of a monologue about how his part of town is not a problem part. It turns out Ahmed is Omar's neighbour, literally. No one would do anything against foreigners who are Omar's guests or Ahmed's guests. Omar insists, and Ahmed nods in agreement, that their honour and their families' honour would protect us. Nothing to worry about! "Well then, why didn't you boys say so…off we go then." The phrase resounds in my head in a very English sing-songy voice: Hi ho, hi ho, it's off to be killed we go…

Hi ho, Hi ho, it's off to be killed we go…

They live off a main road in walled-off homes. Their front road is a small dirt road parallel to the main road but separated by a divider two cars wide of what should have been grass and trees, avenue style, but is now just scrub vegetation, dust and waste. We park the car and get out. Kids play in the dirt. This must be a good sign. Many years ago when I used to hang out in LA and drive around I was told it was cool to park my rental car anywhere there were kids outside playing as this meant the likelihood of drive-by shootings was less there. I wonder, does the same hold true here? There is a corrugated iron shack a little further down the road with smoke coming out of it. We drive by it later and are told it's a hash shack. Looking inside there are a few older Kabulis, dressed in more traditional outfits, huddled round a small fire with a few sheeshas. It reminds me of an ice-fishing cabin. The fire casts dramatic shadows on their well-cragged faces and I have a *National Geographic* moment.

The houses each have a courtyard, poured concrete mostly, with some small green space for a tree. In front of the house, where perhaps a North American house might have a garage, is the "front room." It's here that guests are entertained. We were never given access to any of the actual homes on this trip, only the front rooms, and we never saw any of the wives or sisters. Which I have to say was at times a touch weird, like you're in some sci fi novel where all the women are dead or captured or something. They are just so very absent in certain situations that the oddness of it screams out loud to your senses, and I wonder do other Westerners who come here feel this too?

The front room is just an oblong-shaped room with nothing in it. Well, almost nothing. In Ahmed's there's a built-in cabinet that looks very old and worn. As do the rugs on the floor, as do the curtains and everything else. Central Asia may once have been the Centre of the Universe but all its grandeur seems to have disappeared, to be replaced by 1970s home furnishings that are then never to be replaced, destined to just keep fading away more and more each year. We're sitting around the room on Tajik/Afghan style kurpuchas—cushions about three feet wide and ten feet long and two inches thick. The large cushions ring the room

so we can all have a place to sit large and room to spread, with throw pillows for arms and backs and propping one's self up as one sinks lower and more horizontal as the smoke does its work. I wonder at the way men sit. Some sit small, scrunched in on themselves, legs crossed tight. Here men sit large—legs spread wide, arms back and relaxed. Here men take up a lot of space, which comes off as very macho. There is much testosterone in the room—there always is around here.

Friends arrive. One is an ex-commander, of what? We never asked and are never told. I'm wary of asking too many questions about what people do now or did during this war or that war, and not just in Afghanistan. I'm overly cautious about making faux pas or snubbing someone's honour, and since no one is volun-

teering any additional information, I decide it's best to be less inquisitive than I really am. Another of Ahmed's friends is a very rich guy—you can tell by the way he's dressed and the way he sits that he thinks he's important, which usually means the guy isn't important, just rich enough to have delusions. This one lives in Ukraine, near Odessa. I've been interested in Odessa for some time now and would love to see it. I tell him this and I'm cordially invited to come and stay with him. There is great smoke to be had there and the women are beautiful and easy. Nice to know…

Moving on, we're introduced to a few other friends, one of whom invites us later in the week to his place. We're not scared to come, are we? He laughs. I look at him and say we are guests of Omar's and you are his friend, therefore we are your friends and we feel no fear. (Hinting heavily that if anything happens to us it'll be on Omar's honour as we are his responsibility.) Honour is important here, still. It is not a weird concept for fairy tales and fantasy stories as it is in most countries and most people's lives, but something almost tangible. People here live and literally die for their honour, so I thought it prudent to intimate that we understood how things worked here and were all friends. In my head I'm thinking, "Are you M-A-D? I'm so not disappearing into some suburb with you to go to your house…at least not without Omar and our get-away driver!" Of course later we do almost exactly that and I remember on my last trip I went off with some random guy to go find an antique door to turn into a desk. Only realized I might have done something daft after we left the city. But I'm still here.

We'd forced Ahmed to stop by a roadside fruit stall on the way to his place so that we could pick up something. He was insisting that we didn't need to bring anything but we both told him that it was OUR culture to do so and that OUR honour would not let us come to his home without bringing something to share. And seriously, I'm an English Indian Persian African Canadian—NONE of my cultures allows me to visit someone new without taking something with me. Ahmed stopped insisting—if it's your culture, then by all means. Afghans are VERY civilized in regard to others' traditions and rituals. Is it odd to think the world could learn a few things from them?

We discussed what might be good to eat with tea and sheesha so Oliver and I decided on a watermelon. No, not because it goes well with a sheesha and cake but because they looked so damned good and it was November! When we get to Ahmed's place and are all

finding places to sit and saying hello, he passes the melon through some long curtains in the back corner of the room. A short while later a pair of hands emerges from the curtain with a large tray full of nicely sliced and arranged watermelon. That's the closest I come to seeing any female member of anyone's family—one pair of weirdly disembodied hands.

As the lads—and they are total lads in the UK sense of the word—as the lads fuss and muss with the sheesha and the pipes, etc., the mysterious hands behind the curtain proffer many other items. Tea comes through, along with small bowls to drink it from—piyalis is what they call them, same in Tajikistan and, strangely, the same in Gujarati…but perhaps it is an Arabic word that has fallen into our family's common usage. Many words are similar to me, like dil for heart, bucha for children. I really should research the language trees

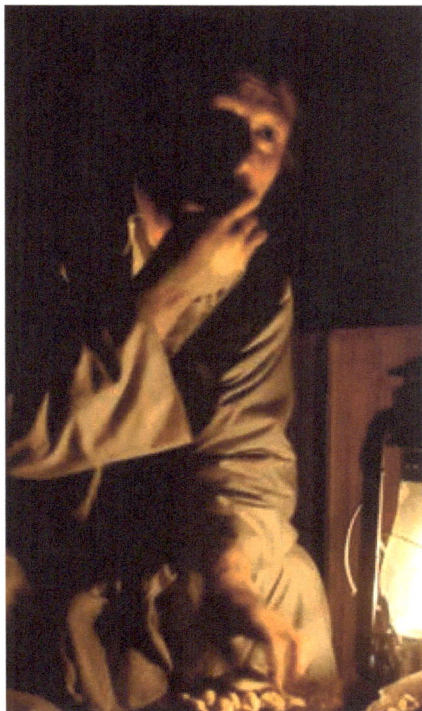

93 - Writing

around here. I'm picking up 20 percent of the conversations, mostly just the gist of things. The hands reappear with a platter of cake—dry and a bit crumbly, it has a very thick, very sweet layer of solid icing on it. There is also the prerequisite plate of dried fruits and nuts.

More rearranging of plates and cups and hot sheesha coals that come out in a brazier so we can finally get the sheesha going. They've filled it with the Arab tobacco mix, which contains fruits and molasses. The mixture is placed in a ceramic holder like an egg cup. Cover that with foil and seal in the tobacco. Taking something sharp like a pen, you make holes in the top of the foil and then connect the ceramic holder to the rest of the sheesha—there are holes in the bottom, small enough for smoke, too big for chunks of tobacco. The coals go on top of the foil, the heat is drawn down into the tobacco by someone sucking on the pipe, which is connected at the bottom end of the sheesha in the glass bowl part that's full of water. The tobacco burns, gently, and the smoke is drawn down the pipe and into the water so it's both cooled and filtered by the time it reaches your lungs. This isn't some

small puff on a cigarette, this is a long draw on an Arab pipe…fruity coolness, tinged with tobacco hits my lungs and I visibly relax—shoulders down, smile on my face. Omar comments and laughs at and with me. "It's been two days since I had a smoke! Leave me alone!" I grin.

As the pipe is sent around the men, the curtains part once more and a small boy is pushed through them. He's Ahmed's son and dutifully he goes around the room giving proper, respectful hellos to each of his father's guests. He's shy around the foreigners, especially Oliver, but he does as his father bids him with a bashful smile that is so Disney-esque in its sweetness. This kid is going to be a looker and break many hearts! Then he's promptly handed back through the curtain into those hands—his mother? Sister? Auntie? Who knows. The pipe's back to me again and I'm sitting cross-legged. Long hair around my shoulders, inhaling and becoming wrapped in billows of smoke. The sheesha is nice, I like it better than cigarettes or cigars, but it's still tobacco and that stuff just makes me a bit zoo-ily lightheaded. Everyone's grinning at me as I pass the pipe along to Naim, who is sitting next to me.

Naim is an interesting guy. He's got a couple of kids and we get to meet them later. He's a hash smoker. Daily, constantly, he smokes. Never quite understood what he did for a living, some type of store. His friends all tell me he is the "strongest" hash smoker in their group, and this is where we learn his father's bi and would love Oliver's blond hair. I look over at Oliver to try and figure out how he feels about maybe meeting Naim's father and I laugh and turn back to Naim who is grinning at me as he hands me a chunk of Afghan Black. "For you," he says, "for smoking later." He smiles, I thank him, one toker to another.

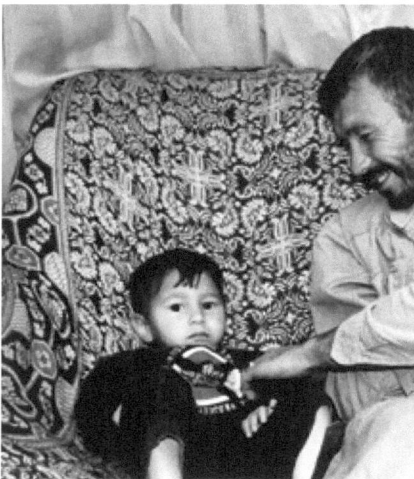

He knows. He understands both my desire and need. We both have the same vice and really need no words, just as Ahmed and I didn't earlier in the garden.

Now that the showing of the kid is done and the refreshments are out and the sheesha is going nicely and we're all a bit relaxed and grinning at each other, what do we talk about? What topic is appropriate to a very conservative, religious and restrictive culture? What do these men, the ones who hide the female members of their families, want to ask two foreign lads?

And here it is, folks: Which countries in your travels have the best women—the best girls for fucking and the best girls for marrying?

These two categories are very separate to these men. We are told a few times that there are Russian and Chinese prostitutes available all over Kabul, including in the Serena hotel. Not in the Aga Khan's hotel? Surely not? But of course they are there…they are everywhere I travel, all over the world they go to make some money. It's the same all over Kabul too.

But, someone adds almost conspiratorially, of course they cost more at the Serena! Omar knows a great place and the others agree, it's a good place. The girls will let you "go" twice for only fifty US dollars. And remember the minimum wage is less than that a month...so the gang we're hanging out with is rich and not just rich compared to other Afghans either. Oliver is a freelance photographer, I'm a freelance writer and project manager, yet these guys are richer than we are but they'd never understand that. We're Western.

This topic of conversation—which women are good for fucking—lasted for bloody ever. I've no idea what to say and the idea kinda grosses me out a bit, but I have friends who tell stories and I read so I just make up some stuff—I'm good at telling tales so I do. Oliver participates and probably sounds more knowledgeable about the topic than I do. It's all very weird. This was not what I was expecting to talk about. It's crass, rude, disrespectful in many ways but to them it seems okay as we're

95 - Writing

talking about non-Afghan women and of course we're talking about girls to fuck, not to marry. It does seem to me as if they've all been cheating on their wives or fiancèes constantly, but of course it's not considered cheating here or in other parts of the world for that matter. The idea that their wives and girlfriends are anything but 110 percent faithful to their men will never even cross their minds. They can do what they like to whomever and however because they are men. It's just that simple: a double standard. Women, even in countries where they are legally equals, just don't get anywhere near the same freedom.

I'm really getting tired of the conversation: there are great prostitutes in Odessa. There are really good ones in Kabul too but the Chinese ones aren't as good as the Russian ones. Well hang on now, another friend disagrees. The Chinese ones are better, they know how to treat a man, not just his member. They are more polite and willing to go a little bit further. Am I really hearing this? Am I really a part of this discussion? I start looking around. There is almost nothing on the walls, they are white, well, were, once upon a time. Now they are stained and yellowed and old and cracking. In the cabinet that holds the sheeshas (and there are half a dozen of them) there are also a couple of Qurans. On one wall is a large poster-size piece of calligraphy done in a gaudy, gaudy style, all gold and shiny. It's some passage from the Quran I'm sure. I can recognize the first word in the first line: Bismillah, "In the name of Allah." That's an easy one to spot. In the name of bloody Allah can we get off this topic of conversation? I'm dying inside…begging the Universe to make this all go away. It's so weird, so incongruous, so just not fun anymore and yet it continues.

They are a very curious bunch these guys, they really want to know answers. We talk about women from South America and France; Thai prostitutes vs. Chinese; Korean women vs. Westerners; all the time it's the same information they want. Who makes the wildest women in bed? We never do come to a conclusion. Which country makes the best women for marriage? Well, that's easy: Afghanistan, of course!

Back in Dushanbe we'd gone to the Tajikistan International Film Festival and seen an Afghan film. It was about two American soldiers, a captain who was white and an enlisted man who was black. It got major applause and the director and writer and film crew were all there in Dushanbe being celebrated and fêted but the film was dreadful, an absolute piece of crap. From the writing to the acting to the direction, it was all, to me anyway, horrid. The cinematography was great and the music neat and the very fact they were able to make a movie at all deserves applause and kudos, but the content was just wrong.

In one scene a group of women walk single file through some desert. The Americans are hidden behind a dune watching them, trying to figure out if they are really women or if they're Talibs in disguise. Then the black soldier goes nuts. He can see the ankles of the women and turns into a stupid horny teenager. No, worse—no American teen sex film has guys that go as nuts as this guy does. He makes oodles of rude comments and salivates and writhes about in ecstasy about the prospect of female flesh—all from having glimpsed an ankle. An ANKLE!

Is this what the Afghans think we're like in the West? Maybe. This whole women/prostitute conversation has set me off just a little. Is this why we can't take a photo of a wedding party? Is this why I can't wave at a couple of kids in a car? Is this why the burqa found acceptance here? Is this why women are removed from society? Are all Afghan men depraved animals who just want to fuck prostitutes as often as they can? Are they so sex-crazy or sex-starved that they can't imagine anyone else not wanting to fuck their wives or sisters if they get a glimpse of an ankle?! Does the glimpse of a woman's ankle really turn them on so much that they need to go out and find some whores? Bloody hell!!!

Doesn't one first ask, "How may I help?" before buying a fleet of trucks?

As we finally get ready to leave and say our goodbyes, Omar tells me again that Naim's father would have loved Oliver. Apparently Naim's father is really, really into blonds and maybe we'll meet him later in the trip—did I see Oliver shudder? GRIN.

Ahmed has been dutifully waiting for us listening to the radio while we're in yet another meeting. It doesn't sound like Arabic (which is what Dari and Pashto sound like to me) and it's not. He's listening to Iranian radio— Persian. We get back in and head to our next destination. He weaves in and out around cars like an expert. The man has a lead foot and I'm not sure if I should be scared because he does look like he's in control and he does look like he knows what he's doing. Besides, I sure as hell don't want to be behind the wheel of the car, not here and not in ANY Asian country! He tells tales of driving a taxi in Tehran (hence the radio station) and makes it sound like driving in Kabul is dead easy in comparison. I guess it is as the "rules of the road" seem to be only suggestions here and I'm not even

sure if there is a Ministry of Transportation yet. There wasn't the last time I was here. If you had a car and could afford gas, you drove. Some German NGO had given Kabul 250 traffic lights, which back then was just daft.

There was no electricity in the town, let alone cops to worry about who was doing what at an intersection. There are cops now; they stand in the middle of traffic, waving their arms around and accomplishing nothing. If they would shoot a few people that might work here, but waving and pointing, yeah, um—no.

Oh and the daft gift of traffic lights is common. I don't mean specifically lights as gifts, but donors giving aid agencies and countries things that just don't make sense. I heard one agency got a donation of some jeep-type vehicles to help with off-road food-aid delivery. Nice idea, but the place the food needed to go to had no roads and is quite mountainous. Much better if the donor had instead purchased a herd of donkeys and hired guys to mush them along. The donor of the trucks of course gave no money for gas or maintenance. Are people really this stupid? Doesn't one first ask, "How may I help?" before buying a fleet of trucks?

I'm far away now, dreaming about how to get donors to pay attention to needs, how to coordinate this and how to "monetize" my role in it all. Do you like that word? It's a new one to me along with "capacity building," "outward-facing," "mainstream" as a verb and a few others. I want to say that language out here in NGO land gets massacred but I'm not sure that's the image I want to use, as so much out here get massacred. Yo! You writer/editor types reading this: what am I trying to

say? The jargonistly twisted English used out here makes my brain hurt sometimes. How does this one grab ya:

"*Mines and explosive remnants of war (ERW) can be described as 'negative investment' or 'investment in reverse', since they can permanently detract from the physical, human and social capital.*"

No…really? Permanently, you say? Wow, big surprise. And what exactly is "social" capital? I figure "human capital" means humans, so basically, "Mines bad for humans" is I think the gist of it…. sigh.

We're in the middle of three lanes, going fast as usual. There is a large median and another three lanes of traffic going the other way. This is one of the new roads and it's nice and straight and smooth and not bombed to crap like so many of the others. I'm lost, dreaming about language and idiots and such, when I notice the car on our left starts to slow down as does the car in front of us. It's a sudden enough change in speed for me to notice, to break my reverie and make me pay attention. Ahmed sees an opportunity to move us ahead so he pulls into the now vacant lane on our right and steps on the gas. He's going to pass on the right, which is a no-no in North America but as I said, there are no rules here. I can see in Ahmed's body language that he's got that race-car driver stance, he's about to let his car out for a burst of speed and pass

Messrs. Slowpoke. He gracefully manoeuvres the car and the gears make nary a sound and instead of the speed I'm expecting, we too slow down, BUT FAST!

From time to time on this road there are breaks in the median to allow traffic to cross, turn or U-turn. Some of these breaks have lights and cross streets and others not. We're slowing down because across our path is an army convoy from the oncoming lane crossing all of ours as they turn left into their army base. The other cars must have seen this and were slowing down to let the convoy pass. Ahmed has slowed our car but he's still moving forward. Like many drivers he's positioning and edging up so that he can be first away when the flag comes down. But this is not the time and certainly not the place for edging the car up. The cars in the other two lanes are NOT edging up, they're stopped dead. Hmmm…stopped DEAD…ahem, Ahmed!

We're now in the curbside lane and there are several guys in fatigues all brown and dusty, not patchy green, because this isn't a jungle but a desert high in the mountains. A couple of them are in the other lanes, controlling and stopping traffic, and a couple on our side. They're facing all ways and watching and they have their guns at the ready, just in case. None of them are paying much attention to us as we edge forward until, of course, one does.

He's now pointing a gun directly at OUR CAR! Holy shit, he's yelling at us and it should be English he's yelling but I can't make out what he's saying. Sounds vaguely Italian. It's definitely not English and he is very obviously not pleased and very highly agitated. Okay, fine…I'm not pleased either, that gun looks bloody loaded! (hell, they ALL look loaded to me) And now he's PISSED OFF! Why? We've stopped! Instinctively—have we watched too many movies?—Oliver's got his hands up as do I. Ahmed is attempting to tell The Soldier with the Gun Pointed at Our Heads that he's not running the road block or trying to do anything bad. At least that's what I hope he's trying to say but he's babbling and getting agitated himself and he's talking in Dari or Pashto or both but it's not English and it's certainly not whatever language The Soldier with the Gun Pointed at Our Heads is yelling in. No life flashing before my eyes, but I gotta tell ya I was a touch nervous. Oliver and I keep repeating something like, "Omar, tell him to put his hands up! Put them up, off the steering wheel! Now! His hands! Tell him now! Ahmed, your hands!!"

The Soldier with the Gun Pointed at Our Heads gets closer and closer and Ahmed's arms finally go up off the steering wheel and The Soldier with the Gun Pointed at Our Heads finally decides we're not a threat and lowers his weapon. Either that or, as the army vehicles had all turned by now, we were no longer a threat? Who knows? And I wonder, since this is an ancient warrior type culture, did Oliver and I just brand ourselves as cowards? Breathing again is a nice unexpected pleasure, and we continue along our way to our next meeting as if nothing happened. I guess around here, that was nothing.

I don't want to meet anyone else this afternoon. I'm pissed off and upset and infuriated and disappointed and fed up. No one seems to care about doing a good job. USAID just paid $8,000 for a job that would have taken my people a few hours to do. Even after explaining this, showing our work, having them ADMIT the quality difference is huge, even then, nothing! No work. It's exhausting to have people be impressed by you, your team, your materials, and then get nothing in return. How can you see my stuff is better and know we are faster and cheaper and still not give us work? Everyone's got a hand out for a bribe and no one wants to hire us. I'd pay the bloody bribes if it would get me a gig but it won't. Because it's not just the bribes—everyone here bribes and is bribed back. The brown envelope is part and parcel of doing work here. I need both the money to bribe AND the cultural/friend con-

100 - Salman A. Nensi

nection. I hear stories from Afghans that what upsets them is not so much the paying a bribe to get, say, a driver's licence, but the fact that you pay and then you don't get what you paid for. And then? To whom do you complain? According to a report from the UN, Afghanis pay over $2.5 billion in bribes a year or about 23% of Afghanistan's GDP!

Too much has happened here. Too much misery, too much of everything…it's a weird combination of high-energy, cut-throat bribes and overpayments and such, and the "we've given up" camp. Very strange to spend your day in that milieu. Oh, someone slap me for using that word!

In between meetings we stop to get some vodka. Ahmed drinks (Omar does not) and we know we'll all be hanging out again soon enough so we agree—get some now for when we need it later. Now I thought we'd end up at the Italian or American PX to buy it as I did on my last visit, and indeed we did look for the US Army PX but to no avail.

There are tons of US Army buildings, compounds, camps all over the place. Driving up to one in a yellow taxi looking for vodka with two foreigners in the back is…well it's just sketchy. I've been in a few sketchy situations and I'm kind of okay with it all but this is really sketchy and strikes me as a touch dangerous too. Wonder what the US guards made of two nutty Canucks in a taxi trying to score some booze in the weird army sections of Kabul. No one we meet knows where we can go to buy booze so—off to the black market it is.

We're now in a residential neighbourhood. Apartment buildings in a group, some single family dwellings and parking lots in between. It looks very North American. We pull into a parking spot and this handsome young man comes over to talk to Omar. We figure on some surreptitious passing of a bottle and US funds ($28 for 1L of booze), but no. The guy is not suave at all—he's uncoordinated as hell and we don't have exact change. Omar pulls out a $100 US bill, and back and forthing goes on with change and bills in full view of anyone watching. Does anyone else think this is a bit nuts?

I've said before that the guys we meet here are all rich…they are but they don't think they are because they compare things to the West. They earn money from doing all sorts of stuff—everyone here has their fingers into as many pies as possible and so this, and the culture, leads to them having cash in hand. So Omar pulling US$100s out of his pocket is no big deal to him…bloody big deal to me, Oliver and I are scraping coinage together for most of this trip just to make it to the next plane or hotel or train. I'd certainly love to have a wad of US hundreds in my pocket!

So the Black Market Guy makes change and disappears for a few minutes, and I think, because I've been in this situation before, thinking the same thing in too many different places, "Is this where we get kidnapped? Or will he take off with the money?" It's happened before—not the kidnapping thing, obviously, but the taking-off thing. I remind you of the adventure Azim and I went on in Dhaka a few years back where we ended up with a rickshaw and no rickshaw-walla…Anyway this young lad does return with the one-litre bottle shoved down the front of his trousers. Not exactly inconspicuous. How did he walk back and ensure the bottle didn't slip through to the ground? The guy then has to make a big palaver to get the bloody thing out of his pants and into Omar's hands! All the while I'm looking out the car window thinking what a lovely sitting target we make.

Transaction done, booze acquired and we're off again at breakneck speed back to the guest house. While Oliver goes in to put cameras away, I walk with Omar around the corner to the local version of a 7/11. It's right on Wazir Akbar Khan—the main drag, traffic is zooming past, guards are everywhere, only a very few people are walking and we have a normal shopping experience—well normal enough for here. I'm still looking around, watching what I can, trying to be observant without being observed. I wonder how the spies do it. In spy movies, the main good guy always has an amazing sixth sense. His training has made him into something with computer sensor abilities. He can see a small shadow and know it's a gun and act accordingly. I try to do that too. But to me a shadow is just a shadow...so, a choice to make: be scared of all of them or none of them. I choose none of them and start to force myself to relax about where I am and how exposed I am.

We get a bottle of pickles, Iranian style, and some cakes and some cookies and some juice and something else weird looking. Shopping here is fabulous. There is so much stuff available it's strange to think of how many Afghans will die this coming winter from starvation. The foods are all from the Middle East, so you get really nice juices and jams of fruits we can't even afford to buy back home. They have four types of cherry juice, guava and mango too for the same price as orange, and other fruits I've never seen before. I've become quite partial to fresh pomegranate juice and vodka...and the Afghan bread with chillies...and the sheesha and the chunky black goodness...yeah, I could live here for a bit, easily. We spent 400 Afg, about US $7, and get two full bags of munchies

and head back to the guest house to get ready for dinner.

We meet Farhad for lunch. Omar's wedding is this coming weekend and so Farhad, his friend, is going to take us around for two days and be our guide/interpreter, allowing Omar to do his wedding prep duties. He and Omar met a few years ago. Both of them went to Pakistan to learn English and then came back to Kabul to be English teachers. Farhad works for a cell phone company now selling services to large corporations but also associations and organizations like the UN and ministries like the Department of Defence. He's very well dressed, suave and emollient. I'm sure he's a bloody brilliant salesperson. We end up having a chat on the street in front of the kebab house, just like back home. I look down the road both ways. We're on a small side street—parked cars along both sides, kids playing, workers moving stuff and unloading. A couple of guys are talking to an old man smoking a sheesha in front of a shoe store. The temperature is cool, not cold per se but not warm. Kebab restaurants abound and the smell on the street is a combination of meat and flowers and the ever-present dust. It feels normal, safe, yet surreal.

We leave Farhad to go back to work and head over to Freak Street to buy some outfits for Omar's wedding. There are three neat streets in Kabul: Freak, Chicken and Flower. There don't seem to be chickens or freaks for sale on the first two, but Flower Street is the place to go for flowers. Omar's asked us both if we'd dress in traditional outfits and we're both more than happy to. I've got several pairs of kurtas at home and they're super comfortable. A kurta is long pajama pants with a huge waist that you cinch with a long string. The fabric bunches and makes many gathers and pleats

around the waist and down to the knees, hiding any hint of body shape till the pants taper to the ankles. Over top of this comes a dress shirt, with cuffs and collar, so long it hangs to almost your knees, tunic like.

As usual, I'm difficult. I want one made in Afghanistan, not one made across the border in Pakistan like so much here. They offer us a selection and we both choose with the help of Omar, the storekeeper and the other hangers-on. Oliver's is much nicer in both design and fabric. Both are light brown and tan but Oliver's has brocade trimming and the fabric looks stronger. Mine is plain and simple and lighter in weight but mine is made in Afghanistan so that's the one I'll take. It feels weird to be walking down a street, going from shop to shop, wondering who is watching, are we safe, who are these salespeople. It's a constant back-of-the-head thing—you're always

wondering and worried. I'm watching out not only for myself but also for Oliver. I'm trying to ensure no one is following or those that have clocked us with the tall blond lad are still sitting in their roadside stalls and not reaching for their cell phones the second we walk past. The endless vigilance is tiring.

Oliver is proving to be quite the hit in the stores and elsewhere. His hair is like a beacon and I wonder not for the first or last time if we really shouldn't have made him dye it in Dushanbe. The store clerks are all very eager to help Oliver. The two suits together cost about US$40 and, well, you take a look at the picture of Oliver, he looks like some Italian noble businessman out of a Marco Polo film! Totally a Venetian salesperson having come to Kabul to trade...

From here we're off to meet Fawad, a Pakistani national who is running a small travel agency here in Kabul. We're buying our tickets from Kabul to Baku, one of the few direct flights out of Kabul. Of course there is the prerequisite cuppa sweet tea. Fawad is brilliant, like so many of the people I've met out here. He's well mannered and so soft spoken you're forced to listen attentively. We sit in the lobby of his travel agency and talk for a bit as the tickets are being prepared.

He's from the Swat Valley, a region in Pakistan that was, until VERY recently, independent; it has a special relationship with Pakistan. Over the few meetings we have with him he describes it and it sounds like paradise. Swat is at the top of Pakistan where it meets up with India and Afghanistan. The region is mountainous but Swat is rife with rivers and valleys whose beauty will make you stop for a moment and just stare at the pictures—stunning. Since I sipped tea with Fawad the Swat Valley has been in the news far too much. The place has been taken over by the Taliban and the Pakistani army has carpet-bombed the place over and over and over. It's just a bloody nightmare over there.

Fawad's family seems be have been rather well connected—he tells stories of playing with the royal family's children when he was young.

Swat had a king and princes and still does even though they are now officially part of Pakistan. Fawad tells us that he was once kidnapped and held for ransom for days in Swat and so now he always carries guns when he drives back home. As he was driving home one evening, a car pulled up behind the one he and a friend were in and he immediately knew: trouble. The car chased them, a second showed up and one pulled ahead of them, trapping them in between. The cars, just like in the movies, swerved sideways and forced them to pull over. I'd tell you more of his tale but he's writing it down and bits of it can be found online. The place he's from has been taken over by those looking for a place to hide from the world and so he says he'd rather be here. Imagine wanting to work in Kabul because it's safer than the place you're from!

Ahmed and Farad come by in the evening and grab us for Omar's wedding. Oliver and I are both dressed in the traditional clothes we bought and I think we look rather smashing. There is a picture of me somewhere at the end of this evening. My beard is full on and full of white; the Afghan cap is jauntily off to one side and I'm wrapped in a warm wool blanket…I

don't think it looks like me at all but it certainly looks Afghan.

The wedding hall is on the outskirts of town. There are lots of them. Large halls, decorated and ready for weddings. This one is covered in neon lights. It's nuts, it's like the lights of Blackpool on acid—so bright the night sky around it is lit up. We arrive at the entrance and Farhad escorts us to a table past a whole bunch of guests. There must be 400 men and boys on this side. Because of course there's a dividing wall that stretches the full length of the room, right down the centre: a six-foot-high, two-feet-per-panel, fold-out, pink divider. Women and girls on one side, men and boys on the other. The band is on a raised platform and I think they can see over the wall but apparently that's okay as they're the band. Some families, we're told, have started having co-ed weddings. Indeed, the one in the other

hall on the other side of the parking lot is mixed. You get the impression that those holding co-ed weddings are considered a bit off... weird people. Sure they're the weird ones!

The young men here are all wearing jeans with tons of doodads on them and T-shirts. I saw this a great deal in Korea and then China and now here. Trousers and jeans with extra straps, buckles, zips, etc., all really doing nothing purposeful, just decorative. Sometimes it's cool and sometimes it just looks daft. Two of the guys are in hoodies which I didn't expect. A bit too American Gangsta culture the hoodie, no? Oh wait, I thought it was a young guy in a hoodie but the guy's my age...holy crap, I'm a middle aged man! Okay, two things. Someone go tell him that he looks daft in his hoodie and doodaded jeans and—oh, crap, I too have hoodies and doodaded jeans in my wardrobe. Oh dear. Someone tell me when the hell did I too get old? Better yet, DON'T!

So like I was saying, most of the guys my age are all in suits—and they're all shiny. Shiny suits, shiny shirts, shiny ties…oy! And the older guys, well they're dressed like Oliver and me. Are they happy about the fact we're dressed like this, or offended by us? Dunno.

Oliver has his camera and starts taking pics. He shoots the old men at their table and we together suss out who's in Omar's family and ensure we get pics of them as we're giving him a web site and wedding photos as a gift. The place is filling up but nothing's happening. Kids are running all over as they do in any country except Singapore and there are even some little girls running around too. Apparently it's okay for them to be on this side of the divide while they are pre pubescent, and Omar's male family members can go on the other side, but that's it.

The band is playing and it's loud. Too loud for me as it's all screechy and sounds to my ear like Bollywood music gone horribly wrong. But the atmosphere is a good one and people are very happy and celebrating—sober! There are many people who want to come and say hello to us; we're at one of the front tables and

conspicuous. In twos and threes they come, for an audience with the Blond One. They vie to sit next to him and then are too shy to talk. They nudge each other and smile at Oliver, batting eyelids. He's oblivious. It's hysterical. Some of them don't speak any English at all, they just want to come and sit near him. I wonder, as with our poor friend Larissa in Korea, if anyone's going to pluck out a blond hair for a souvenir. Oliver is very popular. I'm a touch jealous.

Omar arrives with his father and uncle and they make the rounds, shaking hands, being congratulated. Omar's super-pleased to see us and asks us how we are and if we need anything and if we're well taken care of. It's his wedding day, but that Afghan hospitality is front and centre and it's sweet. We wish him and his new bride well and Oliver takes some pics of him and his dad.

Then the dancing starts, on the carpet in front of the band. By the wall separating the genders the men gather in a circle. About twenty of them, Omar's friends and family.

Most guys stay in their chairs by their tables, but for the ones who are dancing this is the shit. They clap and sway and move in a circle and one by one they enter the middle and dance their own style, their own moves, and all in celebration of Omar and his wedding and then dance back into the circle.

It seems the more you cavort and contort, the more honour you are doing Omar. So they dance, the young lads, suggestively, seduc-tively, sexily, by themselves in a circle of other guys. Hips grinding and bodies slithering ... combine this with what we call the Indian bhungra Light Bulb Dance—you know, where you move your hands like you're screwing in a light bulb, one hand above your head and one by your side. Sexy? HELL yeah—but all the girls are on the other side of that pink wall. I've heard 70 percent of Afghan men are bi; I look at the uberly suggestive dancing and won-

107 - Writing

der who's being turned on by whom. Shake my head, have a sip of water and let the mind be boggled. Weird world.

At one point the kids are all mucking around and Oliver decides it would be good to take some pics of the kids together. So he tries wrangling them into a circle so he can shoot but no, the kids just want to crowd around him and make faces into the camera. Oliver gets up onto a chair so he can get a good angle on the kids. I'm watching him and the kids from our table, sort of as I talk with others and suddenly Farhad flips. I see what's going on—Oliver's head is now above the pink dividing wall. I rush over but he's clued in too and gets down off the chair…phew. The look on Farhad's face gave me a solid fright. I hope none of the guests are offended.

We recover and Oliver, true to his indomitable spirit, does a dance for Omar's honour and happiness. This is good as I'm far too shy and Oliver's a good dancer, he used to pole dance at a gay bar in Seoul but that too is another story. Omar is on a chair, we're all in a circle around him and it feels very much like an Indian wedding except there all the girls would be dancing the way the boys dance here, while the Indian guys would be drinking Johnny Walker Black and Perrier!

Omar leaves the hall with his dad to go eat in a separate room with his new wife and her immediate family. We never do get to see the wife or any of the female members of the family. Guess this is the way it's done here. But as soon as Omar's gone, the food arrives and it's plentiful, varied and good—roast chicken, kebabs, naan bread, rice with mutton, three vegetable curries, plain rice, salad and a few other dishes that were succulent and rich and but I've got no idea if they were even meat or veg. Oh and the chilies— fresh, crisp, with a zing and a bite. There are so many plates of food that they are now stacked up on top of one another. Ahmed is having a great time going from dancing to eating and back. The mood is brilliant.

We finish up and head out about 10 p.m. because we want to get home before it's too late, it's a security thing. Out into the main road we stop and pull over so Oliver can take a shot of the wedding hall. It's very late, very dark, and we're on a weird road with cars flying past. Ahmed is not so into stopping here like this as he's worried about our security and is making decisions on his own because Omar is not with us. Oliver's out with the tripod fast so Ahmed kind of has to go along with us. The shot takes some time as Oliver's doing something with apertures and light capture and such—he's trying to shoot a building at night that's covered in neon. We wait. Ahmed tenses visibly. He's worrying me now. Usually he's super cool. This road reminds me a bit of Highway 7, not far from where I grew up in the north part of Toronto: a highway that's now built up on both sides with strip malls and gas stations and anonymous low-rise buildings. Like North York, like Toronto, I think to myself…yeah, just like Toronto, only AFTER the Americans forcibly come for and get our water!

Oliver gets the picture and we're back in the taxi. Pretty soon we hit a road check and men with guns want to know who's in the back. Okay, Oliver and I are in the back but we're dressed as locals and we're wrapped in wool blankets because it's bloody cold. Flashlights and guns in the face and he tells us to open our blankets—slowly. We do. The guard decides we're cool (mostly I think due to the blond hair as Oliver's hat has come off) and

we go. Home. To the nice hard bed that has no guns pointed at it.

Today is the photo shoot with Hewadwal and Oliver. We show up mid morning, and Omar is with us, even though it's the day after he got married. We rib him about not seeing to his new wife and already buggering off with his friends. He asserts that we are still his guests, it is his pleasure and honour to show us around and his wife will understand.

We leave Ahmed at the construction company and climb into their very large black SUVs. There are two SUVs, a smaller car and a truck in our convoy. Everyone seems to have a gun except Oliver, Omar, me and Waheed, the engineer. I'm pretty sure even the driver is packing. We head out to an apartment building complex that Hewadwal is building. There are four phases and the first completed apartments are already occupied. They're a neat company; they've gone out of their way to ensure community space, clean water recycling and such. Waheed seems fascinated by the concept of rooftop gardens, a particular like of mine. We talk as Oliver takes pictures of guards and buildings. We drive around the whole building site, making sure we have photos from each phase. We pull over when Oliver asks us to—it's his "eye" directing us today, and out of the flatbed truck

jump three guys. They're assigned to protect Oliver and me but I encourage them to take point over Oliver. They move around him in a triangle, each one scanning 180 degrees in an arc that ensures he's always covered. He moves, they move...surreal.

Hewadwal build roads too and works in other provinces also. We talk of their projects, marketing, communications, Requests for Proposals and Requests for Quotes and such as Oliver takes pics. One of the last sites we visit is the fuel storage depot near the airport. HUGE above-ground tanks, several stories high, rust red. They're just going up on the side of a mountain. I wonder what's on the other side? Fuel tanks are a major target but I'm assured it's okay, the Department of Defence is on the others side. That's good, right? From the mountain you can see down into the valley and, so the theory goes, anyone coming at you aiming to blow up the tanks. Good theory. Glad I'm not there to see it tested because the road up here is lined with chemical and other hazardous-type companies. Seems to me you blow up the first one good and proper, and the resulting chain reaction takes out the mountain side. Hmmm...does anyone else out here think these thoughts?

The sun's beginning to go down and we head back into town. Hewadwal wants us to put together a proposal to visit all twenty of their sites and properly photograph each one. Sounds good to us.

Next time Oliver is here he really should play soccer. He's a goalie and out here there are soccer players everywhere. There's no grass or greenery, just goal posts hammered into dusty mud. But there are players nonetheless. One large "field" we pass has at least four, maybe six, games going on it. I'm sure we could have pulled over and gotten someone to let Oliver sub for a few. Next time.

We had another "Now what?" moment with Omar earlier in the week while getting a Bluetooth dongle for my computer downtown from an Afghan service provider. We're in the offices, waiting while Omar explains what we need. He disappears with the clerk (another friend) for a bit and we're left there, waiting again—and wondering. Omar's believes that if

we go to places foreign people don't normally go, we should be just fine. He also asserts that since we only recently got here, no one knows us yet or what we're about so we're not likely to be targets. Relax. Well, Johannes, our UN friend, told us of two French volunteers who got kidnapped right from the airport—someone knew they were coming! Omar also thinks that only important or rich people get kidnapped, but the UN types tell us stories of people being kidnapped for as little as $1,500 US ransom. So now the kidnappers are using foreigners as an income source and not necessarily for political pressure. The Indians tell me it's okay for me to travel to the North but Omar's mum is too scared to let him go. And Johannes drives down from Dushanbe to

Kabul in a UN convoy yet some people tell me if we tried it we'd be a target with the Blond Hair Lad with us. I mean, who do you believe? What do you believe?

The guys drop me at Fawad's office; Fawad's the travel agent, but he's also a major ISP hardware provider out here and I want to talk to him about some infrastructure bidding I'd like to do as part of a communications plan. We need to go to his other office for that information, so we walk out the door, down the street, cross the road to his other place. Sounds normal. Well, it is and it isn't. It's Kabul. There are people milling about in robes and kurtas, no lights, dark shadows, car horns, yelling—and it's fine. The whole trip turns out to be fine; nothing happens to us, but listening to everyone and their stories you can really work yourself up into a frenzy.

We head out again to the guest house to break bread with Omar and Ahmed. Ahmed has brought his sheesha with him. It's safely secured in the trunk with bungee cords, because it's a big one, like mine, standing three feet tall with all the bits and bobs attached to it. The guest house staff love it. They're running around getting us plates and chillies and tea and coals, we've got BBQ chicken and kebabs and bread and chilli sauce.

Omar's wife calls on the cell: where is he? Ahem, in a meeting with the guys…home soon, yeah, dinner sounds great. We all look at him. Ahmed starts laughing and so do Oliver and I. Lying already? He splutters and tries to deflect our comments with his own commentary on us and some of our behaviour at a bar the night before. We all end up laughing—it is a great night. Omar's only going to eat half a chicken as he has to have dinner when he gets home! Ahmed pats his tummy and says something in Dari. We laugh too. Sated and sheesha'd, the boys head out, with Ahmed promising to get Omar home fast…I bet! As they're packing up stuff to head out Ahmed lets slip that after he dropped us off from Omar's wedding, he went back and sneaked into the co-ed wedding in the other hall so he could dance with the girls. And here I thought he was gay. He's not gay, he's just randy!

Why? Why is the flight at 8 a.m? Seriously. Up early, packed and double-check all the luggage, pockets, zips, etc. Sim cards exchanged, GPS, phones; hard drives and movies copied and copies of pics. It's a frenzy of admin in the morning but we're well organized. We're on our way to the airport and it's still dark outside.

The town is weirdly normal. Yeah, the guards are still everywhere but so are people on their way to work, opening shops, sweeping the dust from their front sidewalks, having coffee at the side of the road. We're at the air-

my bags onto the weigh scale, but not the guy behind the counter! The old man waving us to passport control also has his hand out. In total I spend $25 US on bribes trying to get to the departure lounge. Oliver, who has fewer small bills on him than I, simply refuses and they give up. I tried to refuse but was hounded so I gave in. Easier. I know I know, we shouldn't

port fast, and the guys bid us a teary goodbye. It's been a zany few days and we're all going to miss each other.

Through the security check and X-ray and then another table and a full bag search, unless you pay a bribe. I have no desire to have all my stuff removed and then have to repack so I slip the guy a fiver, USD. Then the next guy wants a bribe for the pat down; and so does the guy who wants to put plastic straps on my luggage; and the guy who tells me what line to line up in as there are no signs; and the guy who puts

pay and we're fostering the corruption, etc., but bug off, it was 6:30 in the fracking morning! I just wanted done and at our seats which, by 7 a.m. we were in.

If you've seen photographs of the American Midwest during the Depression, when that most fertile of lands became a dust bowl, blowing away farm houses and dreams, then you've seen Afghanistan. After years of drought, soil erosion has beaten away at the country's once-lush fields and gardens. Deforestation from

years of war and an ongoing lack of rainfall have left a desolate moonscape in places that once were lush and alive. With a water system that depends heavily on mountain run-off, the Afghans can only hope that each winter will bring heavy snow. Which of course kills many but ensures water the following spring.

Whenever and wherever conflicts occur, the most able are always the first to leave. If you have money you get out; if you have an education you get out; if you have a religious affiliation you declare you are a refugee and you get out. Once everyone is gone and decades have passed and skills and talents are lost to a whole generation or two, it then becomes hard to attract educated people back. New lives have been started elsewhere and the children no longer know of the homeland in any context other than old stories. Despite this, however, many Afghans have uprooted their families once again to return home and rebuild. I think it takes a certain kind of person, like the old pioneers of North America, to pick up and start again. These people are the ones running the start-up businesses responsible for doing the practical ground work of rebuilding the country.

Everything, absolutely everything—from roads to schools to parks—must be built again. It's hard to attract money for some of these projects, because something as simple and important as a road is hardly a flashy thing for governments and organizations to pour money into. Many of the roads and often buildings too sit literally half-finished, awaiting money to complete the opposite side of the street or the top of the building.

And through all this you can see that the spirit of the people endures, is not gone... it is diminished, tarnished, battered, bruised and in many cases beaten into a pulp, but it's still there. Through the drought, life goes on. Through the violence, life goes on...and the Afghans seem to just get on with it.

When you think about it, what other choice do they have?

Salman A. Nensi
Kabul, Afghanistan

KEEP YOUR HANDS AND FEET INSIDE THE VEHICLE! (NEPAL)

by Salman A. Nensi

Welcome to the New Republic of Nepal

"Please keep all your limbs inside your vehicle, lest a taxi driver separate you from them!"

I've been in Nepal for about two weeks now... The friends I was staying with, Johannes and Munira left on Saturday. I was going to get to stay in their house for the rest of the month since the place was paid for but the landlord had other ideas... literally minutes before they leave the country he decides I can't stay and makes some fuss about security... what he meant was, "I've already rented the place and I want to collect double the rent for two weeks!" Yeesh!

So with much insanity on Saturday I'm now staying with a lovely couple, Amelee and Filipo... Filipo is head of UN security here and they are from Fiji and the sweetest couple... Amelee even showed me where the secret ice cream stash is in case I need some in the middle of the night... as you do! LOL. They have a tonne of kids, I'm still not sure how many but then I've been at work all day for the past three days so haven't seen anyone really. And yes, I've been at work... those of you still sniggering can stop now! Thank you very much, I do work from time to time and I work damned hard... just not into the whole 9-5, Monday to Friday thing so many of you seem to be enamored / trapped with!

* * *

I'd forgotten some of the things I love about Kathmandu... the quiet at night is sweet... until the dogs set each other off... but it is still quiet... you can hear the insects and feel the breeze... it's sweet... just not the nighttime feeling in Western cities. Maybe it's just me? Other things I've missed were buffalo and chicken pickle... yeah really. You know the Indian style (Patak's) mango or lime or garlic pickles, well here they do the same thing in the same way but with buffalo meat or chicken meat... how insane is that? Well, not really, it's bloody yummy! The limes here are tiny, like the size of radishes and the tomatoes are not that much bigger... but the taste is sooooo sweet! 'k nuff about food. Anyone want more info on food just ask, I could go on about the markets and the fruit and and and, it's not Thailand but it's still pretty good!

People here remember me, which is nuts cause it's been two years since I was back but I guess I make a bit of a ... how to say it? Ahem, I guess I take up a bit of space! I used to go daily to this Japanese body balancing place, method is Sothai... and it's brilliant. When I walked in two years ago with Mun, who had just given birth and wanted some massage, the guy looks at me and says, "oh dear, you've come just in time" and proceeded to give me daily sessions for ten days... and I swear I walked taller after each one. On the way home from a session I'd stop by the German Bakery and buy some cookies 'cause as I walked home I'd have a nightly smoke... which meant Mun and I had tea and cookies when I got back. Very civilized.

The practitioner, Toma is back in Tokyo studying but his mother and father remember me... as does the guy at the German Bakery as does the guard, the night guard, the nanny and the maid! I can't believe they remember... the maid, Indira, said to me it's like I've only been gone a few weeks, not years... and you know, she's right, feels that way to me too.

I find Kathmandu very comfortable. Even with the noise and messed up driving and smells of diesel and rotting garbage; the crooked roads and sidewalks that are mere suggestions... I walk against the traffic so they can see me coming... everyone else walks WITH the traffic so I'm causing a bit of a problem due to my size and the smallness of, well, everything else! Mini busses stop in the middle of the road to let old ladies off straight out into the screaming traffic... and everyone ambles... they just seem incapable of moving fast... I move faster reading a report and watching where I step... twisting an ankle her is a real possibility with every step and you learn quickly not to step on anything that looks like a man hole... what's the PC term for that again? Human Egress Panel?

The other side of this place is the green, the mountains, the mists, the warm rains, the quite nights, the smells of food and bread and flowers on the air... sigh. This morning I saw what I can only describe as a Council of Dogs... there were like 30 of them, in a field, all kinda sitting and paying attention to each other... was bizarre... tried to take a pic on my phone but we whizzed by to fast. And I still haven't figured out to get the pics off my phone but that's another story.

And a note on the weird stores out here... DVDs matched with used office chairs and today I went to get money transfer from a Western Union and it's a local affiliate that handles remittances for expat Nepalis sending money home and they also sell.... TEA! So anything smaller than 5NRs you get in tea!... could be worse, in Kyrgyzstan they give you soviet crappy candies instead of coins.

Last weekend we went to the mountains... they're not really far away so it's like Vancouver, 'cept here the roads, like the sidewalks are mere suggestions... you get real Western type roads in town for a bit but then they're mostly made up of the same red dust bricks they build their houses out of... the type that are crumbling AS you cement them together... so the journey can take a while and is always a bit of a bone cruncher. Traffic is nuts cause everyone is more interested in avoiding the pot holes than staying in their correct lane... and you would be too if the pot hole could swallow a diesel BUS!

Johannes drove... and he'd be a great Formulae One / Crash Derby driver... he's well into the traffic and how to drive around the ever infuriating Nepali drivers... they stop in the middle of the road, they change lanes without signaling, motorbikes are weaving everywhere and people just cross the road without even looking or caring... it's a bit crazy making and Johannes is like me... a bit vocal when driving. Apparently we only have to worry if he starts swearing in Turkish...swearing in any of the other half dozen languages he speaks are ok though!

Mike, you would so not approve of Nepali Building Codes! The houses and shops are amazing looking... Peter, last time we were here, called it clumpitecture and that's the best word for it... Houses just have bits added to them willy nilly... a balcony there, a room build off the side of the third story there. It's as if bits were stuck on with glue, totally without a plan... zaney. There is a reason... Nepali inheritance law gives all male kids an equal share, unlike Korea where the eldest lad gets it all. So what happens when the house is divided DOWN THE MIDDLE? If you want to put on a balcony you put it on only your side... same with a room or if you want to turn it into a shop, you do and your brother house, well looks like clumpitecture!

As you wind your way up into the hills the annoyance of the city fades and small villages built of the same red dust bricks are now surrounded by rice paddies of the most vivid shades of green... which is saying something out here where there seems to be several hundred shades of green everywhere you look. The Kathmandu Valley is lush in a way that London, New York, Bangkok are not and perhaps never were... well maybe Bangkok was... There is nature here in all it's glory and softness (is that the right word) everywhere. Some friends are moving to Bangkok from here after being here for 15 years... they are going to miss the green of here tremendously and they know it. There are cows milling in the street, dogs lying everywhere and half naked kids playing in the massive puddles left by the warm monsoon rains that show up with an intense furry and last sometimes for only 10 minutes. It really is sweet.

Joh and Mun took me along saying it was just a place to chill for a night... turns out to be a major resort type place, part of the Le Meridian chain and the ex Prince has a space on the grounds. I didn't know so I packed light and felt like a git 'cause nothing I had with me didn't have holes in it! (Miranda, you can tell Uncle Bill I thought of him BIG TIME!) He's always giving me grief for looking like a bum! Did you show them the pic of me in a suit? I used to hunt every Friday morning, when in the UK, for clothes I could wear to breakfast that wouldn't get me yelled at... Thought I had it once and then got yelled at for not untying my shoe laces before taking them off. Hee hee... I do miss Uncle Bill and Aunte Marlene tremendously... t'is one of the best things about being in the UK, having a proper English Fry Up every Friday morning, David you are often talked about and well missed!

So here I am trying to figure out the least offensive / most posh combination of tatty rags I call clothing but really I didn't have to worry. It's monsoon season here so the place was virtually empty except for staff and monkeys... everywhere! Up close and personal, they're a bit scary... they look so amazingly human... but smarter... well smarter than the staff at the resort anyway. The staff try to keep them away from guests and food, etc... but give me a break, the space was theirs long before the resort showed up and they know it... so the staff tries, but the monkeys always, ALWAYS win... it's fun to watch.

The room was massive... bath tub like a Roman bath, space for at least 6... 150 channels on the TV with complementary CAKE in the room! Yummy too and the room was larger than a Canadian living / dining room. All to myself it was a bit much actually.

Sheesha (chillum, nergileh, hubbly bubbly, bong whatever you want to call it) is brilliant outside, under an awning when the rain is POURing down in sheets. (wonder where the monkeys go?) Mun and I stayed up far too late and chatted about life the Universe and, well you know... so amazing was the evening that it actually made me a bit sad.

I know... but it did.

When I went traveling the last time I was only planning on going a few weeks... and it was years before I made it back to the place I'd left... this time I knew I was going and I knew I didn't want to go alone... for those of you part of the Winter of Stupid you'll know I thought I had someone 'special' who was up for joining me on the next journey but alas, things did not pan out. And while planning this trip, none of my friends was able to say they'd come with me this time... lives, wives, partners and kids; mortgages, careers, retirement funds and new cars... these things are not conducive to buggering around the world for months / years at a time. So I had a choice plan to go alone or not go at all. Well, that's not really a choice at all now is it?

There I was, end of the most perfect evening... with the most luxurious room... and alone and a touch sad. So I had a little sit down... a little smoke of the good stuff... and had a wee think on things grand and small.

Here's what I think... I love what I do, really I do. I love the fact that I get to see what I get to see and be where I get to be and that I can do this without needing to ask permission or put something else on hold or be moaned at yelled at told no, etc... all things I have heard my friends dealing with over the years when they have desires that do not conform to whatever has become the 'norm.' Traveling and seeing the world has become part of who I am, it may or may not always be a large part of me but it is right now and I love it. Therefore, just because there is no one physically to share it with should not and in fact, does NOT diminish the awe of what I experience nor the joy I feel being out and about. So... onwards... n'est pa? GRIN

* * *

In Tajikistan when I worked at the UN offices for a week I was called the Mullah from Bhukara. I had one week in which to accomplish what I needed a month to do and so I put in an 80 hour week. Those of you who

have experience me in HYPER MODE will understand why I got the title of Mullah... I got what I wanted out of whom I needed to get it out of, that's for sure!

It got cold in Dushanbe while I was there and I needed winter clothes 'casue I wasn't prepared and had brought not much warm cause I'd never thought I'd be in Central Asia in the Winter! I went and bought local... a very long, to my ankles, quilt coat of brilliant green... very Harry Potter but t'is the thing out there. I also got a small green hat for my head (some of you got versions a few years back)... well that hat is from Bhukara (every region / valley has it's own hat style and the taller the hat the more important you are—to us Western types, the taller the hat the MORE Monty Python you look but hey, this is why we travel... just make sure to never laugh at the 12 year old wearing the HUMONGOUS army hat... he's not 12 and he's got a gun bigger than hid hat!)

I tell you this story to say that I get nicknamed everywhere I go... Some of you know me by one or two or even three names... I have 7 or 8 now that I answer to depending on where I am in the world and whose doing the yelling. Here in Nepal's UN office I am called... "Mr. Bollywood" I think it's cause of the hair, see attached picture, and my thanks to Bill for the neat photo shoot this pic came from. Which brings me to another reason I like it out here. By "out here" I mean any place NOT totally Westernized... Here, I am seen as a person whereas many times in the West I feel that I am seen as brown first, and a person second.

I know that sounds a bit dumb... it's 2008 after all... but perhaps those of you with accents or skin tones different to the majority around you know what I mean. It's not overt acts of racism that I am talking about... those are few but I prefer them to the subtle way many Westerners, especially in the dating world, make you understand that you're not white and so you're just a tiny bit second class. Unless you're in the UK, then they just call you a Paki and chase ya!

Considering the multi racial / multi religious group I grew up with in Toronto, it took me far far longer to realize what was being thrown at me by so many. I kinda assumed everyone had a group of best friends like mine: some Jews, a couple of Christians, a Hindu... a Korean, an Indian, a Brit and some 'Canadians'... naively it was a while before I figured out most people don't have that. Which is a shame cause as kids and teens we got to go to EVERY feast day with all our friends... and when you combine the faiths, there's a tonne of feasting going on every year! Maybe that's why I'm such a foodie?

But back to Mr. Bollywood... The Resident Representative for the UN has three secretaries... one of them who is a bit older, wears a sari and sits right outside his office can't look at me without smiling... it makes me blush! She's old enough to be my mum... but then again, looking at who I choose as my partners, I'm one to talk, eh! LOL

As vain as it is, and I know it is... I really like being in a place where Hollywood doesn't dictate what is interesting, attractive and worthy.

* * *

Sunday was Gai Jatri... festival of the dead. Also, in older times, the one time of the year when Nepali's could use satire and 'festival' to comment on or mock those who ruled... so of course this is the day chosen by the Blue Diamond Society for the sixth annual GLBTI Pride Day. Yep, Nepal has a Gay Pride Day and the Supreme Court has ruled GL BTI people are "normal" and should be accorded all rights... they're even leaning towards allowing gay marriage here! Dunno why it's Blue Diamonds instead of Pink Triangles though. (Pink Triangle, Blue Diamond, sounds like a box of Lucky Charms instead of Fruity Loops!) I can't believe that this bloody acronym of GLBTTQQII and whatever else they've decided to add has followed me here! In Toronto it's now like 11 letters long!!! Enough of you have heard me rant about this silliness but just to say it again, why can't anyone who's ever had even a queer thought cross their brain just be Queer and lets get on with living life? Maybe cause, by my definition, 90% of us are Queer? Well, I do think we're all a bit queer... maybe some more than others, naming no names! Grin... Oiy Miranda, where's that pic of the lovely and queer Ross?

I was at the office for most of the day but I did pop out for the parade... I had been invited to an open house in Baktipur... pur must mean town or area 'cause there's lots of places ending in pur here which is why I didn't clue into the fact that Gertz and Ludmillah live in a DIFFERENT TOWN!!! I should have clued in when the cab driver wanted 1,000NRs just to get there (xe.com for conversions but about 65NRs to the Canadian... bout 140NRs to the British pound.) Taxis are exorbitant here... partly cause gas is now 110NRs a liter!!! And there isn't any to be had. Gas lines are a full day or two long and you are only allowed a few liters. Black Market gas is available but at 250NRs per liter... Diesel is 85 a liter and home fuel about 65. And in the West you think you pay much! Think of what a Nepali earns in a day and then try to see how you'd buy oil for your home, let alone gas for your car.

Back to Baktipur... (gosh I digress a lot, sorry)

I finally got an old guy in a beat up cab with no windows and no seat belts and I was sure he was going to hand me a spanner just in case my seat came away on the next bump... but the old guy took me for 400 waited and hour and brought me back. We spoke all the way there about his kids and the country and state of affairs... seems most people I talk to want their king back... and the monarchists have four seats in government so one never knows. There is little to meld these people into one nation with nationalist pride. The monarchists want a constitutional monarchy so that the people have something to rally around. Quite weird watching a feudal society transform itself into a republic in 2008! He spoke to me in Hindi and I spoke back in Gujerati... was quite amazing.

Back to Baktapur... Gertz and Ludmilla are amazing. They've been here for 30+ years. They're home is a typical Nepali courtyard house... and it's 260 years old! Lovingly restored and cared for it is a maze of stairs and rooms and gorgeous carved wood everywhere. Luke, can't wait for you to see it, you'll want to photograph it all! From the outside it's just a plain wall, small cobbled street and all very nondescript. Inside it opens up into something from an ancient history book. The garden... oh I can't even do it justice. These guys built the Garden of Dreams in Kathmandu and it is the most serene, interesting and well kept garden... it's like them and their home, full of joy and life and celebration of just being.

I met a gaggle of ladies who have all been her 20 years plus... and in fact the one who's been here twenty years said it as if she was a bit ashamed she's only been here such a short time! There's a Canadian lady who is now 91 and has lived in Nepal since 1954! Anyone seen the movie Tea with Mussolini? It's about a gaggle of English ladies living in Italy in the thirties who just don't believe that war is coming. These ladies aren't that naive but they have a certain feel about them... they love this place so very much and it shows.

However, things change and change fast. One of them just lost the ancient house she was living in... why? Developers. I kid you not... the land in Katmandu Valley, especially in the city itself is expensive and getting more so ever hour. So these gorgeous houses, that are hundreds of years old, are being torn down to make way for? FLATAS!!! Apartments!!! And Office buildings! BLECK! Take a guess as to how much a good size piece of land will cost here... big Western style home with a garden... have a think, tell you in a bit.

Baktipur is an old town... the streets are tiny, the houses ancient, the bridges, waterworks, town square all in these red brick... it's a maze of walk ways, cobbled lanes, hills and water... I know I'm not doing it justice but perhaps when Luke gets here his pictures will... it is TOTALLY a place I wanna go back to and chill for a bit to soak up some of the atmosphere.

The parade was a blast to watch said everyone... I was at work so I got there well into the parade and the entire area around Gert and Ludmilla's place was parade... there were tones of guys dancing with sticks that they smash above their heads making loud noises... kinda like dandia for those who know what that is... pictures of loved ones who have passed on alters decorated and held up by four 'pallbearers', guys dressed in dotis or saris, girls dancing and singing, music everywhere... it is a loud, joyus, insanity of sound and colour and emotion. I didn't get to see it, I was bloody IN IT... for at least half an hour as the parade and I wound our way through the small cobbled streets as people threw water and flowers. I almost missed the two small stone lions that mark the entrance to their home! Was a blast... totally.

* * *

A few days ago I told another friend I want to go to Bhutan... this got me an invitation to a dinner with the Ladies from Bhutan... all zany all funny all unable to handle the drink and all here to gamble! That's what rich Bhutanese do... they come to Kath to party! Bhutan, I am told, is only 700K people... and I can't wait to see it. These ladies are connected... one of them is a Minister in the Kings government and another is the sister to the King's press secretary. Bhutan's king just abdicated in favour of his son who is slowly modernizing the country but slowly, pro6ooperly, with care as well as he can for his people. His father forced his people to accept a constitutional monarchy when they didn't want one. An interview I heard a few months back had Person on the Street Interviews with Bhutanese saying they would vote, but only cause the King asked them to! He apparently surveys his people's Happiness once a year... just a simple question, Are You Happy? If the number goes down, the Kings' ministers are in trouble. How simple is that?! Yo Mikey, wanna try that in Ontario? Think George'd go for that? lol

Anyway we got talking about food and cooking, as I often do... and I find out that Bhutanese cooking is all bout chilies, vinegar and salt! How is it that I never knew this before? Well I know now and so Luke and I will be taking a 'class' with one of these crazy ladies as there's no cooking school to speak of in the capital. There are however fields of smokables EVERYwhere... and indeed in Nepal it is part of a ceremony once a year to celebrate Lord Shiva's birthday... but strangely it is a day of fasting. So you're supposed to smoke all day and NOT EAT... now that's commitment to your gods!

In the middle of all the Evening with the Ladies, I get enthusiastically invited to a party in November if I can make it back... the Ladies insist I be there and join them early for the festivities as they will be long and hearty. Never one to shy away from a party, especially if the food is hot and spicy, I'm totally in. I wasn't sure then I'd be here in November but I'm in. Curiously I ask what the occasion for the party is, assuming a marriage or festival. Nope, it's the new King's Coronation party! YIKES! Never been invited to a King's Coronation party before!! What on earth would I wear! LOL!! But alas, by November Luke and I will be far from here and so I'm not sure I'll be able to make it back even if I did have something to wear, which is a real shame cause the country fascinates me. Check out their latest stamp, done by a company in Pittsburg, it has the five kings of this dynasty on it and has a CDROM in the middle of it!!! I so want one. Anyone want one mailed to them on a post card? I can't remember which of you is a stamp person. (Don't worry Jason, I'll pick up some currency for you, hope it's as cool as the stamps!)

Luke, I am so glad you decided to come out to see and play... I know some others of you are talking about it and I really do hope you can make it too. As I type this the rains have descended and the loudness is amazing... I might just finish up for now and go for a stroll in the warm downpour....

Life out here is not normal to be sure and it is not always safe and certainly not easy... but it is LIFE in a way that you just can't get in Markham or London or Welwyn or London... hee hee, did I say London twice? Those places have their charms, sure... but for me, this, this out here is LIFE in all its glory and pain. And I am content again.

* * *

Some of you wanted to know about my work... well it is both amazing and infuriating... I am so sick of UN acronyms I'm ready to shoot someone, so are the people working on this gig with me! The UN is a big organization that is also like a medieval country with each agency acting like a jealous lord all ganging up on the king from time to time and all fighting each other for money and power... it's kinda weird actually considering what they stand for. But I've done this before and so am navigating the politics and diplomacy and getting what we need to get our job done is happening... just making me a bit nuts as it does. And yes, I CAN be diplomatic when I want to be! lol. And what we are learning and seeing and helping accomplish is tremendously rewarding after a career in the soul sucking Canadian publishing industry. Here things matter... for real they matter and if you fuck up, people die... it's as simple as that. No pressure, eh!

I have a nice office space... it's a kinda cubicle but a bit more than that... kinda like an office but a bit less... so very Nepali! LOL. I have a wonderful view of the mountains and the tea lady bring me masala chai on a regular basis so what's not to love. Well the constant saluting and calling me Sir might have to stop... okay not the saluting but the Sir makes me feel old! lol

A few days ago I was on the roof with the lap top working away when I get an email from my friend Jon... he's in Japan, heading from Tokyo North to his wife's parent's village for the weekend on a bullet train... emailing me... and my phone rings, it's Dileep, calling from some Asian airport as is his want. And as we chatted, I emailed Jon back, sipped my tea and thought... wow... how on earth did this happen?! The net is a neat thing to be sure. And yes, Jon and Akemi are married... and Dileep and Miew are expecting a little girl in mid Oct!

* * *

So what's next? I think I'd better fill y'all in on the plan for the Fall in case any of you guys really DO want to join Luke and I on any of this.

From here to Bangladesh on the 2nd of Sept (assuming I finish this UN gig and get paid!) and back here on the 11th just before Luke gets here. We'll do a week or so in Kathmandu, Baktipur and Phokara before flying to Bhutan do some cooking and temple seeing and well just BEING at the top of the world and then flying back to Kath

Then we fly to Lhasa, Tibet and chill for a few days while learning how to make MoMos (John, if I make it back to Canada I promise to make some for you!) and then we'll take the train through the Khashgar pass into Kazakhstan. I have a few friends who used to live there so we're hoping to score a free empty apt as Almaty is a pricey place. Kazakhstan has oil and gas and has done for some time. It is a RICH Central Asian country. We'll do a weekend there, see what the night life is like and then head overland to Bishkek, Kyrgyzstan.

I want to head into the mountains a bit and chill by Lake Issy Kul (home of the best smoke in the region I'm told... but that statement doesn't include Afghanistan!) There's also an old style BBQ restaurant that Azim took me to when I was there last that I want to revisit. T'was very rustic and you'd be hard pressed to tell what century you're in when eating there!

From Bish to Dushanbe, Tajikistan where we'll meet up with Johannes and Munira and the kids again (and they can have their stuffed animals back... not enough luggage space so Hippo and Lamb are with me and Charlie and JJJ) Charlie is my teddy bear, JJ is his younger, cuter better dressed bf! A no I'm not to old to sleep with my teddy so SHUT it!

In Dush we also will hook up with Lois, a fabulous friend we made in Seoul. She is the new school principle at the school Mun wants to enroll Lara in... how neat?! And our friend Anise from London may be there also. We'll chill for a bit and meet up with more old friends and drink too much Georgian wine. Then we head down to Kabul for a week. Flights in and out are only on Saturday so we'll go for a week and fly back the following Saturday.

I had wanted to spend a month touring the Afghan north and the west but am told things are not so good as they were in 2005 when I was there last so we're listening and planning accordingly... so those of you who are overly worried, stop. Not doing anything too nutty! Okay?

From Dush we'll fly out to the Uzbek border and spend a week driving the old Silk Route and visit places like Samarkhand (a fabled city from stories I read as a kid) to Tashkent to Bhukara (where I'll get another hat!) to Khiva (have started a book called The Road to Khiva, published in 1876!!!) and across the border into Turkmenistan. We've got a cooking class in Bhukara to learn proper pilov a staple dish of rice and carrots and meat... very hearty, very yummy...

A few days in Ashgabat should do us and for those of you who remember Nathan? The 6'5" Aussie we picked up last time I was out here... sorry, another side bar... Typical Aussie Nathan was going from Athens to New Delhi to catch a flight home, only he wasn't going to fly he was going overland. We met him in Dush and dropped him in the middle of a mountain pass a week later! And you guys think I'm nuts!! Anyway, Nathan recommends another nutty lady with horses, so we're going to see her and her horses.

Hopefully across land to the Caspian Sea won't be too nuts but it's a funny state Turkmen... this is the place where the ex ruler (now dead, his son is new ruler, of course) had renamed the days of the week after himself and his family and there was a statue of himself, in gold, in the city square that turned so he always faced the sun! dunno if that's still there but I hope it is.

By boat next across the sea to Baku, Azerbaijan where another friend we met in Seoul is stationed. We'll crash with him for a few days before flying down to Tehran... yeah, Tehran... why not? It's there and it's not turbulent just now... and well... yeah. Lol

From Tehran to Bangkok... Luke has a wedding to attend on Phuket Island after which I'm taking him to my beach... many of you have been there with me... you know its sweetness and charm. I have had some emails with Eddie from Bamboo Bungalo! And he's well please to learn of our return. Disappointed when I told him our whole GANG isn't coming this year (He remembers us all!) but I hope that some of you will join us there for the holidays.

Luke will take off back to Canada Dec 13th and I'll probably do a small side trip to Yangoon, Myanmar or Vientiane, Laos (both?) and then head to Singapore to visit with Dileep and Miew, Nathan (their first child) and the new arrival, sorry Deep... I forget her name. And then I'm off to Melbourne for a few quick days of fun with old friends and finally... finally back to New Zealand, where I hope to stay for a good solid chunk of time... and if I like it this time as much as I did the last, I'll start the paperwork to emigrate. Followed by a nice long streach on a boat cruising the South Pacific Islands cause after all of this, I am sooooo gonna need a break and some serious chill time.

So, whose coming along?

Let me know if you want off this mailer... I'd like to write to you all individually but there just isn't always the time, please accept my apologies... doesn't mean I love you less! Grin. I'd also like to say I'll write weekly but you know me... it'll come when it does. And sorry but my camera's broken... good think Luke's coming with his so just pipe down we'll get some pics... meanwhile there's always Google Earth!

Lastly... that piece of property in downtown Kathmandu... it went for $2.5 MILLION DOLLARS US!!!! I kid you not... two point five million!!!

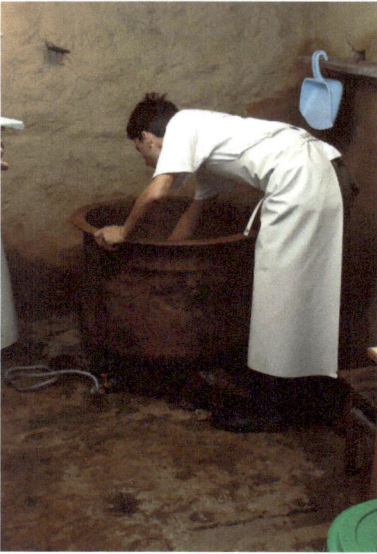

Almost like his native writer Jules Verne's classic *Le tour du Monde en Quatre-vingt Jours* (Around the World in Eighty Days) where two intrepid souls set out to circumnavigate the world in 80 days on a fully wager, François Delard of France, too, travelled the nooks and corners of the world for three consecutive years in the capacity as a reporter of a business magazine. He traveled to 30 countries across the globe after finishing business studies from the universities in Paris and Barcelona. But at the end of the day, he realized business studies was not his cup of tea and rather looked for a 'platter of cheese.'

Like every Frenchman, he grew up with bread, butter and cheese. He had a deep-seated passion to do something on his own. When he came to Nepal, firstly, he made a point to live in this country, and secondly, to earn his bread, butter and cheese, he vowed to do something cheesy.

"I had a romantic idea of making cheese here for the reason that milk is everywhere. And secondly, I wanted to start a business without doing any harm to animals," François recounts the reason d'être behind his Himalayan French Cheese Pvt Limited, a cheese factory he has just established in the idyllic hills of Chandeshwori of Tokha village to the northwest of Kathmandu.

He established the cheese factory by collaborating with three of his Nepali friends on a small scale. He then went to the Savoie Valley in the French Alps for training. After his return to Nepal, he has been manufacturing the traditional French recipe with Nepali touch.

"We follow exactly the same procedure as they do in France, known as 'Tomme de Savoie'. Since Savoie is a place in the Alps, I don't hold the right to give the same name," François elucidates. "We call it Himalayan French cheese."

François has eighteen cows in his shed in Chandeshwori where four Nepalis, besides him, work to look after the cows.

Two women cut chunks of the curd day in and day out whereas two men milk the cows and assist François in cheese making.

Cheese making is a laborious enterprise, as it involves maturing of cheese under impeccable conditions up to three months. The semi-firm, disc-shaped product is put in a cellar or a cave with the humidity of 95-98%, and the temperature of 10-14 degree Celsius.

This process comes foremost that give the cheese a thick rind with rustic appearance.

"These are the fungums that give the cheese taste," François explains, showing his cheese. "The cheese must ripen in the cellar, these molds are indigenous and harmless."

However, many Nepalis are not accustomed to the taste of the cellar. Thus, his clientele mostly comprises French and expatriate community in Kathmandu.

The other reason for his limited clientele is the price of the cheese. François explains, "This is basically a farmer's cheese. In France, a kilogram of 'Tomme de Savoie' costs between 17 to 20 euros. It seems like a luxury there, and the masses go for industrialized cheese which costs a lot cheaper."

Himalayan French Cheese is available at some of the premium outlets to Kathmandu, such as European Bakery (Baluwatar), Delicies (Bhat Bhateni), Chez Caroline (Saber Mahal Revisited), and Herman Helmers (Jhamsikhel), among others, with the price tag of 1,650 Rupees per kilogram.

"I hope it'll take less time to go to Nepali clients," François adds, "Some hotels are also approaching us at present."

With a considerable success in his cheese business in a short span of time, François is all set to take bigger strides in the coming days.

"Nepal is a land of opportunities," he adds after a contemplative pause. "Every week, I pop out two ideas. I also want to manufacture other French delicatessen in Nepal."

ANCIENT FRENCH CHEESES, KATMANDU STYLE

by Salman A. Nensi with Jon Southurst, Photographs by Oliver Strong

Traveling through Nepal on my quest for more of Asia's best home-style food, I hardly expected to come across a traditional French cheese maker making cheeses in a cave just outside of Katmandu—especially one with such a strong dedication to custom and quality.

Himalayan French Cheese (HFC) is a collaboration between one French trekker, Francois Driard, and three Nepali partners, Binod Neupane, Gokul Magyar and Ram Bahadur KC but business isn't their main agenda. HFC is more a collective of fine food lovers looking only to produce great foods, starting with cheeses. Limited to local materials and supplies they're also subject to local weather conditions, temperatures and energy supplies which in a place like Nepal can be a bit of a challenge. Above all the four food loving partners want to ensure they are enjoying themselves while also creating delicious things to eat.

"Industrialized cheese is no good — good cheese should stink and be covered in mould!" says Francois, French partner and founder. Not so sure about the stink or the mould? Wait till you try what he's created, you will understand that Francois speaks a culinary truth. There is, unfortunately, no shortage of bad mass-produced cheese available in Asian supermarkets at higher prices far higher than HFC charges.

Francois has been in Nepal since 1996, when he came for his first mountain trek. You could say he never really finished it as he keeps finding new places to climb and trek—the Katmandu Valley has some of the most gorgeous scenery in the world, The Himalayas! These days Francois is not camping or staying in guest houses, he has built himself a two story house on a gorgeous piece of land above the city and his very own cave in which to mature his cheeses. (2000m higher would be more ideal, but he likes to stay close to his friends). After starting out using milk from other sources, he now keeps his own herd of 13 milk cows and hires a local cowboy for 12 hours a day to take care of them. Dairy in Nepal is a "weird secret industry," he says, given cows' sacred status in the culture.

Francois doesn't claim to be an expert cheese maker yet. In fact, he'd had no farming or cheese making experience until September 2007, when he headed to the mountains of France for two months to study the art. Making French cheeses is something you can study for decades, says Francois, and still not be an expert. He's learning the old fashioned method —by learning as he goes.

At first, HFC was producing about 4kg of cheese per day, but demand has grown such that they are up to 8kg a day and hope to soon produce about 10Kg daily. His cheese is one the French call Tomme de Savoie— although European Union regulations prohibit him using the regional name Savoie, hence the more relevant-sounding 'Himalayan French Cheese.'

French cheese experts advised him to start with the Savoie recipe as it is one of the easiest to make. Francois plans to return to France to learn a new cheese each year to add to his repertoire and his customers can't wait. HFC is sold only through two locations in Katmandu, the European Bakery and Herman's Bakery. Why there? Francois says they make the best crusty bread in Katmandu, and that good crusty bread is vital when enjoying good cheese. Being French, he also believes wine and cheese go together, "If this cheese doesn't make you want a glass of wine, then it's not good cheese."

All over the developed countries the art of making traditional food is being lost as mass produced, manufactured products masquerading as food take over the grocery stores. How amazingly refreshing to find someone interested in carrying forward old traditions with quality and enthusiasm. Boutique cheeses and meats in the West, if available, have become a tremendous luxury costing many times more than the mass produced alternative. Hand made French cheese is absolutely a luxury in Katmandu but the location and production costs allow Francois to keep his cheese priced at a very acceptable 1250 Nepali rupees or about €12 per kilogram.

Hotels have been expressing interest in buying some of Francois delicious cheese and from time to time a batch is sold to the French Ambassador in Katmandu—a certain mark of Francois expertise and the quality of his creations.

Francois insists that growing the business is not what his enterprise is about. He is, first and foremost, a lover of find foods and would not want his business to grow too big as to not still be enjoyable or suffer a drop in the quality of what he does. HFC has never done any marketing—the taste of his cheese has done it all for him and continues to be his best advertising —try a slice and you too will be asking if he has an extra kilo you can buy.

Francois is already starting to think of other ways to bringing more France culinary delights to his small corner of Nepal. He talks of expanding his farming activities, moving into meats and perhaps even creating a French style delicatessen? With a charming glint in his eye he also talks about wanting to try an elephant milk cheese too! Whatever Francois and Himalayan French Cheese does, it will be done in a traditional way, with style and quality and the most spectacular of settings.

Tomme de Savoie á la Francois

Francois takes me on a trip to his self-built farm in the hills of Chandeshwori, Tokha village to the northwest of Kathmandu, where he creates these delightful cheeses. It can be a little lonesome out here on the hilly outer suburbs but with his staff, partners and dog named Bongo he has created a good life for himself. Being a trekker and climber there is a host of wilderness for him to wander through. His farm is located just below Shivapuri national park, the garden of Shiva. The scenery is beyond breathtaking.

Our taxi can only get so far before the road becomes impossible to navigate and then just stops. A 20 minute walk follows and there's a stone wall that seems to go around the mountain along which you have to walk on top to get to his house. Great in August but I wonder how it is in the snows of Winter. Further up the wall is a temple but the farm is on the left.

It takes about 10 liters of milk to make one kilo of Savoie style cheese and at 8 kg a day, that's a lot of milk. Owning his own cows has proven far better than attempting to source the required quantity of milk every day and he is able to monitor the cow's health and feed—keeping a close eye on the cheese making process from the very beginning.

Francois rises around 5:30am every day. He and his cowboy, Lila Bahadur Tamang, collect about 40 liters of milk every morning (and another 40 liters in the evening). The milk is gently heated in an ancient-looking copper pot. Rennet, imported from France, is then added and the mixture starts to solidify. The mixture is cut and folded in on itself and stirred by hand which with Francois means all the way up past his elbow. At the right time, with the right solidity and right smell and taste, Francois knows it's time to remove the curds and pack them into plastic moulds and weight them down to squeeze out the extra moisture or whey. The whey byproduct has multiple uses including providing a nutritious supplement for local babies and children. Turned and drained the curds begin to form one solid mass and are then placed into the cave, kept as a special temperature and brushed and turned regularly, in order to mature which can take one to three months. Once matured the cheese forms a thick rustic rind that is multiple shades of gray-brown in colour and has a earthy, cave like aroma. The interior is a creamy blend of straw-yellows and off whites that is both salty and savoury to taste and does indeed go very well with a nice bottle of wine and some crusty bread.

Every step of the process, from the temperature of the milk to the timing of the block cutting and turning, is a guarded secret. Not that there is any competition out here, but Francois is a traditionalist and professional who is learning and honing his craft in a very personal and self fulfilling way. When asked how he knows when the curds are ready for the moulds his smile twinkles again, "I just know."

Each week Francois descends from his farm into Katmandu taking his cheeses down to his clients. He drives a 28 year old Lada jeep with no seat belts, no radio, no nothing and he drives it like a Formula One driver on any surface while grinning wildly from ear to ear. Clearly Francois is a very happy man, doing what he loves—making delicious cheese in a most spectacular setting.

For more information about Francois, his cheeses and his next adventures, please visit his web site at www.HimalayanFrenchCheese.com.

Salman A. Nensi is a freelance writer who likes to spend his time eating traveling and eating. Jon Southurst is a writer based in Tokyo, Japan.

NENSI.COM

BHUTAN: SHANGRI-LA WITH CHEESE AND CHILLIES

Photography by Oliver Strong;
text by Salman A. Nensi, with Jon Southurst

The mission to find and eat the most local of local dishes around Asia has taken me to some exotic places. In this case it's one of the most exotic of all —and surprisingly, it didn't even take a plethora of street food options to win me over! I can't say I knew what to expect from Bhutanese food, only that it involved cooking with lots of chillies and melted cheese. This was enough for me. If two of my favourite ingredients are a significant part of the national diet, then I figure Bhutan is the perfect place to continue my mission.

The landscape of Bhutan itself is stunning. But words like *stunning*, together with *amazing* and *awe–inspiring*, really mean nothing until you're standing there yourself, jaw dropping at the vistas and valleys dotted with ancient temple fortresses known as *dzhongs*. Involuntary clichés like *Shangri-La* or *Eden* might tumble out, but it's hard to visit Bhutan (Land of the Thunder Dragon) without them entering your mind.

From the moment you step off the plane, the land's energy seeps into your bones, and you experience a calming feeling of being in the moment, open to everything around. The people, charming and hospitable, are proud of their heritage and culture and can talk about them in colourful detail. The capital, Thimpu, a small town of 40,000, is clean and charming. It's also full of laughter and great cooking smells.

Bhutan, now a constitutional monarchy, is the only Buddhist kingdom left in the world. It had, until recently, an absolute monarchy that had reigned since the current royal family was voted into power in 1907. Despite the best efforts of powerful neighbours and outsiders, it has never been colonized. The current king, Jigme Khesar Namgyel Wangchuck, on the throne since November 2008, is, at 31, the world's youngest monarch. He has maintained his father's plan to improve the lives of the Bhutanese while retaining their strong identity and culture. This country has the amazing ability to pick out only those elements of "progress" it wishes for, and the courage to discard the rest. Thimpu is not Bangkok or Kathmandu and (perhaps thankfully) will always be an alternative to the region's other cities.

Tiny Bhutan is remote and mountainous, with only 47,000 square kilometers (18,147 square miles) of land, but it produces a surprising diversity of local fruits and vegetables. From peaches and apples in the south to hardier vegetables like potatoes and peppers in the north, the local markets overflow with a great variety of produce at prices that haven't climbed as sky-high as they have in many nations.

Local restaurants are mainly family run—always the best kind—and small, with only a few bringing in chefs from outside the country. Although we sampled some terrific Indian, Chinese and Tibetan specialties, our desire was to eat local and preferably street food. Bhutan, though, doesn't appear to get into street food as much as its Asian neighbours. Perhaps it's the size: with a population of 700,000 the vibe is more country town, with no one rushing to grab a quick street meal on the way home. The roads are not clogged with cars and bikes all competing for the Loudest Horn medal, and homes are large with decent-sized kitchens, unlike Seoul or Tokyo where a two-burner hot plate is very often "the kitchen."

Our guide, the fabulous Ms. Chimi, tells stories of dinner parties, pot lucks, and meals for friends given as gifts, and sometimes ingredients are brought as gifts so that people can cook together. This is fast becoming a country I'd love to relax in for a while.

The Bhutanese might not do street food the way others in the region do, but they definitely do food and it's a huge part of the culture. After eating a few hotel and restaurant meals we were lucky enough to get into the kitchen at the Lakhi Yangchek hotel in Paro, Bhutan's second largest city. Head chef Tshering Deema, along with her two assistants Karma Dorji and Sonam Tshering, treated us to two great nights of cooking and learning the ins and outs of Bhutanese cuisine.

And while experienced travellers will tell you that the best food experiences are not usually found in fancy restaurants but rather in street stalls and small cafes, where people who know *their* dishes have spent years practising and refining them, the chefs at the Paro hotel certainly seemed to know their dishes.

From them we learned that the spicing of most Bhutanese dishes consists of salt, chilli, grated *datsi* cheese and ginger. Carrots with the skin still on are also used as a major flavouring ingredient. This is great, since the skins and peels of vegetables are full of vitamins and nutrients.

Datsi cheese, made from yak or mare's milk, is quite mild and pleasant with a nice chewy texture. Its low melting temperature helps it to incorporate into the sauce of any dish it is added to. Prepared in small soft rounds of about two inches across, the slightly thicker rind is sliced off and added to dishes while the softer, less ripe interior is then put under some cloth to ripen so that the next day there is more rind to use in cooking. The Bhutanese produce a few other cheeses, including a rare one that sounds akin to a French Stilton. But as with most things in Asia, foods are seasonal so we'll have to go back when it's time to make and eat those cheeses.

As in my mum's kitchen, all ingredients are added by eyeballing them, tasting what's already gone into the pot or simply having a sixth sense that says, "Add more salt now!" It's a sign of well-honed dedication to the cuisine and dishes being prepared when the chef knows what feels right and can change the spicing depending on the quality, freshness and quantity of the ingredients.

Bhutanese chillies are larger than Indian chillies and significantly larger than Thai chillies. Milder in heat but strong with pepper flavour, they are used in almost every dish. Since Bhutanese chillies are hard to find in Western grocery stores, large, light green Korean chillies make a great substitute if you have an Asian grocery store nearby. If not, a combination of green peppers for the pepper flavour with some smaller chillies for heat might suffice, but you'd have to do some experimenting.

Flash frying or wok frying chillies is wonderful to watch: the flames shoot up over the pan, and the flesh of the vegetable chars while releasing stunningly flavourful oils and smells into the food and air. You do have to make sure the kitchen is well ventilated lest you, and your cooking guests, end up in fits of chilli-fume-induced coughing. Chillies are, remember, the main ingredient in defensive pepper spray weapons.

While we'd been told the Bhutanese love chillies and vinegar, we didn't see much vinegar, which is a shame as my palate says a little tang would have brought out even more the unique and delicious flavours we were experiencing. There were two small Nepalese-style limey lemons in the hotel kitchen and, being a fan of tangy and chilli, I ate both in one meal without realizing that unlike in Nepal, where citrus is readily available, in Bhutan the two small fruit were precious.

Did we mention the salt? The uninitiated should be prepared, because the Bhutanese sure love salt. It must be the high-altitude need for it, because whenever we turned around, head chef Tshering Deema was adding another sprinkle of it. If it wasn't her, the two assistants were ready with pinches of their own to add, encouraging us to add more if we felt the need. The Bhutanese even put salt in their morning tea, just like Tibetans do. Such practices seem counter to everything a Western cup of tea should be.

I've noticed Koreans using scissors in the kitchen in place of a knife, and I have to say I'm with them there; it's much easier for many things to simply *snip-snip* over a pot than to fiddle and chop. The Bhutanese kitchen has no scissors; for them it's a machete with a massive tree trunk as a chopping block. And again, just as in my mum's kitchen, you save your used oil for next time. Just strain out the fried bits for the dog or any family member who enjoys them. Take note of what you re-use the oil for, though. No one should use oil from fish-frying for anything other than more fish-frying, for reasons you can probably imagine.

One of our favourite meals included *sha hint shoe*, a tasty dish made from strips of beef that are first hung outdoors to dry and cure. ("*Dried chillies are best with dried meat.*"~ Bhutanese kitchen wisdom.) The drying usually takes two to three days if it's nice and hot outside but can take from five to seven days if the weather is cooler. As with many cuisines of Central Asia, pressure cookers are ubiquitous in Bhutanese kitchens. Due to the mountainous nature of the country and the historic price of meat, much of the meat here is preserved—by drying or smoking—and is tougher than any beef jerky I've ever had in the USA or elsewhere. Use of a pressure cooker to tenderize the meat and bring out all the flavours trapped inside is essential.

The dried meat is hacked into bite-sized pieces and put into a pressure cooker along with spinach and/or turnip leaves and fresh chillies. Once this is cooked, the *datsi* is added and the whole concoction is heated on a stove top, allowing the melted cheese to permeate all the ingredients, making one with the beef and broth to sumptuous effect.

One last thing to note: these meals should be eaten piping hot, to help bring out the maximum flavour, especially any dish that includes the cheese. Any cheese lover in any country will tell you that melted cheese needs to be eaten quickly.

And eat it quickly we did, because the food was delicious! At the Lakhi Yangchek hotel we were fortunate to come across so many experts in one place all working and tasting and creating together like a well oiled machine. Bubbling broths, charring chillies, machetes hacking and chopping and gorgeous huge open flames to cook over. All are powerful reminders you are no longer in downtown London or New York—this is how real food is made for real people.

Sha Hint Shoe Datsi

Beef with Cheese and Spinach (or Turnip) Leaves

Ingredients:
- Dried beef, 1-inch cubes/strips
- Spinach
- Salt
- Chillies
- *Datsi*, rind
- White processed cheese, cubed

Preparation:
- Overcook the beef in a pressure cooker with oil and salt
- Chop or rip the spinach into bite-sized pieces
- Cut chillies lengthwise and then in half, about 1-inch strips
- Add both chillies and spinach to the cooker; stir in
- Add *datsi* rind and processed cheese cubes
- Cook for a short while without the cover until the spinach wilts and reduces
- When cheese is thoroughly cooked, add salt, of course!

Helpful Hints:
- Use long-leaf spinach and keep the stems as they are considered tasty.
- Wring out all the excess water from the spinach after washing it.
- Try to keep the spinach, chilli and beef pieces all the same size so your food cooks evenly.
- Wash dried beef in boiling water and then cut into 1-inch strips using your machete and a tree trunk!

Salman A. Nensi is currently on this third trip around the globe working as a consultant for development agencies and eating everything delicious he can find. He divides his time between London, England; Toronto, Canada and everywhere else.

Oliver Strong is an accomplished photographer who has spent the majority of his youth savouring the tastes of new places in an attempt to gain some sense of perspective to add to his small town upbringing.

Jon Southurst is an Australian native who has been living and working in Tokyo, Japan, for the past ten years. Jon is never bored as all he has to do is open his front door and revel in all that is Tokyo.

TOAST Á LÁ DOK BUK GEE

by Salman A. Nensi, photographs by Oliver Strong

I had been working late. Hunger drove me to wander from my apartment to go and see one of the local *adjumas* who work around my building selling hot food to Seoul's hungry late night crowd. The variety of foods available from street vendors here in Seoul is remarkable. Afternoons and evenings are the best time for street food, when countless *adjumas* (married, middle aged women) unpack their trolleys. The *adjumas* will serve you everything from fried egg sandwiches (topped with brown sugar and ketchup!) to hot dogs covered in French fries on a stick. Don't be surprised if you find Korean fusion delights grilled right in front of you such as dough pockets slathered in mayonnaise or minced meat packed around a bone. The aromas are intoxicating. It's hard to walk down the street without stopping and buying something, even if you're not the least bit hungry.

I've been to this particular food stand before, a few times and by now Ms. Bo Hyun who runs the stand and I are well acquainted. She speaks no English and I speak no Korean and yet from time to time we manage to have some good conversations and she knows I come here to enjoy her spicy dok buk gee. Hers is a special recipe using extra spices and sweetened with hard candies instead of molasses—making her sauce richer and darker than the other vendors in the area and considerably spicier and I love it. When I first started to come here she was amazed that a foreigner like me could enjoy something as spicy as her sauce. I've caught her talking to her other customers about me and my spice tolerance. She's impressed but I'm just hungry and she's a good cook.

A few weeks ago I saw her making something I had not seen before for one of her customers—A toasted sandwich of shredded cabbage and carrots. It looked good so I asked her to make me one. She grinned at me—she likes it when I try new things—and was pleased to make it for me.

The sandwich starts off with some butter on a flat grill… things are always great when they start with butter! Then the bread is fried, just a little, and then set aside. Poured onto the grill is a mixture of shredded cabbage and carrots in an egg batter. Fried to a golden brown on both sides and carefully shaped into a rectangle the same size as the bread by her expert hand. Placed on the toast it looked great. Then came a healthy table spoon of brown sugar and a dousing of ketchup. I objected to the sugar and the ketchup but was told this is the way to eat this sandwich. Always up for trying new things I shrugged my shoulders, grinned and said okay. Folding the sandwich on a diagonal Ms. Bo Hyun stuffed one end of the sandwich into a paper cup and handed it to me along with a few sheets of toilet paper. I took the sandwich home with me and ate it while I continued working. It was good but far too sweet for my palate.

So now I'm back standing in front of her stall wondering what to eat and I notice she has a friend visiting. An older lady is sitting on Ms. Bo's side of the stall eating one of these toasted sandwiches and they're having a solid chat—acting as only old friends can. The older lady looks at me and says hello. I return the greeting and think she looks familiar. Ms. Bo tells me her friend works at the market downstairs where I regularly shop for groceries. It's so neat to be recognized and share a smile, especially when there's a language barrier. The lady holds up her sandwich and suggests I have one and I agree. However, I have a twist to suggest...

I watch as the bread is toasted in the butter... and I ask Ms. Bo to leave it toasting just a little longer so that it browns up, crisp on the outside with a centre of sweet butter! Then I watch as the filling of carrots and cabbage is shaped and fried in the remaining butter and my mouth begins to water. Ms. Bo's friend is watching me as I watch the cooking process and the two of them start talking about me. I can tell they're discussing me but I have no idea what they're saying but they're smiling and nodding at me. Ms. Bo is asked by her friend if I like the food and is told that I'm here often, usually for the dok. I point at the dok and use one of the few Korean words I know, "mashisay-yo"—delicious! This elicits wide grins and more smiles.

The sandwich is ready, the egg patty is gently placed on the bread and Ms. Bo reaches for the sugar... I stop her. She looks at me and picks up the ketchup, "Want some ketchup?" Oh no... no ketchup either... I'd like some sauce from the Dok Buk Gee but of course I don't know the Korean word for sauce (it's "sauce," by the way) and so I ask for some dok buk gee mul (water) hoping she'll understand and she does. But she's surprised and starts laughing. This is not the way to eat this sandwich and she tries telling me so. I shake my head and insist on the sauce. Pointing to the bubbling dok she picks up the spoon and fills it with fiery red sauce and asks me again if I'm sure this is what I want. I nod yes... I love this spicy sauce—it's going to taste great.

Ms. Bo looks over at her friend and the two of them have a quick chat about me and my sauce and laugh about my weird request. I grin at them both, "It's going to be delicious... trust me... really." I laugh and they do too and still shaking her head Ms. Bo tops my sandwich with the sauce and places the other slice of bread on top. The two adjumas look at me and the friend asks if I'm sure this will be "mashisay-yo" and now it's my turn to laugh—of course it will be. Completing my weird request I ask her to wrap it up in foil instead of placing it in the cup so it will still be warm when I get it back to my apartment. She's still laughing as she does it and her friend is looking at me wide-eyed and I reassure them, "really, it's going to be yummy!"

Getting the sandwich back to my place, I unwrap it and it's still warm and the butter has melted into the bread. I take a big bite and it's delicious just like I knew it would be. Hot and crisp, eggy and moist, smothered in spicy sauce—yum!

It is said that experiencing the local cuisine is a great way to get to know a new culture and its people. I say hanging out with street food vendors is an *awesome* way to get to know a new culture and its people! The *adjumas* in my neighborhood have given me a warm welcome and made my stay in Korea a happy and well-fed one and I know they'd be more than pleased to do the same for you, even if you have a weird request or two!

Salman A. Nensi is a freelance writer and communications consultant who divides his time between Asian and North America. Oliver Strong is a Canadian photographer currently spending a year exploring Korea from his home base on Kungwa Island, northwest of Seoul.

CLIVE BARKER

by Conan Hunter & Salman A. Nensi

"Art is very often a way for us to partake of the ecstatic and the delirious vicariously."

There are the movies: *Hellraiser, Nightbreed, Lord of Illusions, Candyman.* There are, of course, the books: *The Books of Blood, Cabal, The Damnation Game, Weaveworld, Imajica, The Hellbound Heart,* and many others. A legacy of conjuring archetypal horrors and articulatinglating nightmares-forever etched into our culture-measurable in millions of units in prints. And now the novel *Galilee,* which is curiously, subtitled "A Romance."

Has Clive Barker, one of the boldest writers of dark fiction, straightened out?

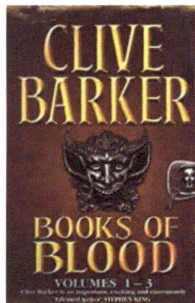

Galilee is the story of two people approaching each other from opposite ends of reality: one is escaping the inner circle of one of the most powerful and influential families in America, and the other wanders estranged from his ancient, mystical family whose destiny is intertwined with the former in a tangle of mystery and doom. Barker takes us deep into the psyche of these opposing worlds, with a tragic, if at times sordid, examination of the human soul in its barest form. Years of cultivating his own inimitable brand of horror, which stood out shockingly as attacking our conceptions of reality with tales of savage surrealistic depravity, have taught him well the navigation of the nether regions of the heart and mind. But in Galilee, this is only an element and not the whole of the story.

Barker has been moving further and further away from horrifying the reader as the goal of a book. *Weaveworld, Imajica*, more recently *Sacrament*, and now *Galilee*, attempt to use his talent for pushing uncomfortable buttons within us to greater ends than just shock. These books are certainly dark and fantastical, but these supernatural worlds and beings are now cast as extrapolations from reality, examinations of reality, and, perhaps at their most ambitious, opportunities to explore our notions of the world and ourselves. "The problem with this horror nonsense is that it implies a simple effect. What is the function of a horror novel? Well, I guess it's to horrify; that is far from what I would ever think of doing with 14 months of my life (which is what it took to write *Galilee*). My intentions are incredibly complex" Barker bristles. "The title of horror writer is almost insulting."

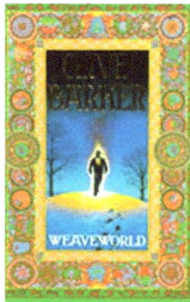

"Dark fantasy has a chance to touch us so deeply and to describe so elegantly the movement between the internal and external worlds, " Barker says in describing his work, drawing attention to the fantastical works of Shakespeare, such as *The Tempest* and *A Midsummer Night's Dream*. "I would like my readers to come away with fresh revelations about who they are because they have been in a magical world."

Galilee, then, is not simply a horror novel. Neither is it a romantic novel with a few magical bits thrown in. The novel uses the two main forces to mirror each other's truths throughout, and it is in this manner that we see the characters' loves and relationships, which is how this book earns its subtitle. Barker's work has always been peppered generously with sexual tensions, which veer into unexpected and often disquieting territory, and *Galilee* is by no means an exception. Yet, alongside some of the most disturbing scenes of twisted sexuality Barker has yet written, there is a powerful and very real love story here.

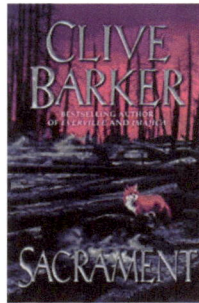

There is no doubt that horror was the main force contributing to the success of the movies inspired by Barker's tales. This has not drawn his focus from his beloved medium, the printed word. "The fact is that books do incredibly complicated things to people because they are operating in conjunction with the reader to create a very individual series of possibilities in the reader's mind" Barker says. "The words are a point of stimulation-they're not the end of the journey, they're the beginning of the journey. And the end of the journey is unique to each reader." Barker views the movies as a way to bring people to his real work. "I think movies are an inferior art form to books, paintings, and music because they demand a singularity of effect at a certain moment: the ship is going down, now cry. That singularity is easy in the experiencing because really it doesn't rely upon you at all, you can be very passive in that situation. I don't think passivity in the face of art is necessarily something to be celebrated."

Is Barker, then, a champion of the word? "I don't think it behooves anybody to be too pretentious about this. It comes down to the simple business of entertaining people, telling people stories that inspire or catch their imaginations."

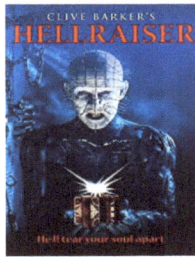

For Clive Barker, a self-described "professional weird person", it is an extremely successful business. His 19 books are now in 23 languages, and there are 10 million copies of his books out there. None of his published work has gone out of print. Each year they're reprinted and new audiences are finding them. "Time is kind to this kind of fiction," Barker says. "Kinder than it is to other kinds of fiction, and kinder than it is to movies."

Perhaps Barker's readers are finding a way to touch their own dark side, as it were, in his work, and this is why so many partake of it. One has to wonder what goes on in the head of a man like Clive Barker, whose output is consistently intense and often disturbing. "The balancing act is to access the edge of our sense of where consciousness gives in to insanity and craziness, to get to that place without toppling over. Writing is a way for me to do that," Barker says. "It's a way to communicate frenzy and delirium and hallucination, and in the communicating of it allow people to access it without having to be put on Thorazine after the experience. Art is very often a way for us to partake of the ecstatic and the delirious vicariously. We have an appetite for that."

Has Clive Barker straightened out, then?
Hell no.

Conan Hunter is a freelance writer living in Toronto. Salman A. Nensi is a freelance writer who divides his time between Vancouver and Toronto.
This interview was first publishing in the Montreal Gazette in July, 1998

GEORGE TAKEI

by Salman A. Nensi

Takei has just finished rereading his autobiography. Rather he's just finished reading the abridgement for the audio version of *To The Stars*. The only cast autobiography to be written entirely alone, his book is over one hundred and fifty thousand words long—the abridgement a shade over twenty four thousand. "If you can imagine the flesh being carved off your body, you can imagine the pain of seeing your life cut down like that. There's just a skeleton left." Said Takei in a recent interview from his home in Los Angeles.

The Simon and Schuster audio version runs three hours—no more, no less. Paring down the book would have been too painful for Takei so his publishers enlisted an outside abridger. Even so, Takei was involved in some of the fine tuning. With a finite amount of space, every scene Takei wanted to keep meant he had to decide which scene was dropped.

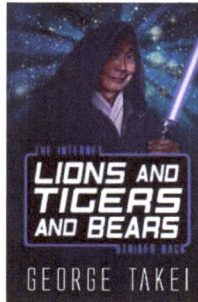

During World War II thousands of Japanese Americans, including Takei and his family, were interned by the American government. Number 12832-C, known to us as Captain Sulu, along with his younger brother Henry, baby sister Nancy Reiko and parents, was taken from his home in Los Angeles and interned behind barbed wire in the middle of Arkansas. "In the bright sunlight, we could see every barb glinting and flashing like sharp, deadly gems strung out along the new wire fence. We passed tall guard towers with armed soldiers staring down at us." The barbed wire gates closed behind the internees—Takei was four years old.

"The internment camp was such an important formative experience." Said Takei that he had them put the scenes back into the audio version. Having spent a number of his early years as an internee, Takei later testified before a congressional hearing which eventually led to President Reagan signing the redress bill which gave each surviving internee $20,000 for their pain and suffering.

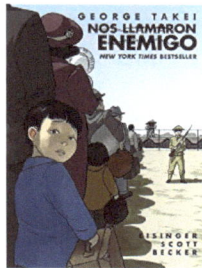

Takekuma Takei, George's father had once said that justice is neither blind nor fair, it only reflects society. It took fifty years for reparations to finally be made but Takei still thinks America is moving towards becoming what its rhetoric states it is—only the movement is slow. "Justice was awfully tardy. My father had pasted away by that time. So he died not ever knowing that there was going to be an apology and in our family it was my father who suffered the most."

"I'm optimistic enough to think that we do learn from history. And then, at the same time, we don't learn from history. When Desert Storm broke out I was chilled to read in the *LA Times* about the FBI visiting Arab American community leaders. The indication in the article was that there was no rational basis for that other than they were Arab Americans. A few days after that there was another article in the LA Times about an Arab American grocery story in West Los Angeles being fire bombed." Takei is convinced that irrational behaviour by governments encourages the more unstable elements of society. He sees a definite cause and effect and called a press conference to draw attention to his conclusions. "That's exactly the way it happened to Japanese Americans—the FBI coming to visit community leaders. Then it was sabotage, today it was terrorism."

Takei still believes humanity will win out. After almost thirty years as *Star Trek*'s Sulu, he can hardly do otherwise.

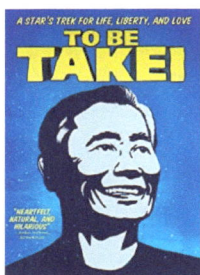

Takei is quite candid during the interview, he is equally candid in his book. "I certainly wanted to correct certain fabrications that effected my integrity. I also wanted to deal with certain illusions that some of my colleagues may have about themselves." When asked how he's preparing for the inevitable reactions that will follow publication he replies, "I'm eagerly girding the loins."

Almost from the very beginning, Takei and Walter Koenig have been friends. Over the past thirty years Koenig has kept Takei informed of every come-back rumour, every casting change, every story idea, every plot twist (both on and off the set). Every phone call began, "Guess what..." In a recent Guess What conversation, Takei found out Captain Sulu's daughter gets to meet Captain Kirk. "It's intriguing. I'd like to know how I had her. Who her mother is. That's the thing about doing a long lasting serialized film or TV series. You really are in the hands of the writers and the other moulders and shapers of the series. You make your input and you hope for the best. In my case my input didn't take too much during the time I was there [Takei is not in *Star Trek: Generations*] and I'm so delighted to discover that I was so ultimately productive after the fact."

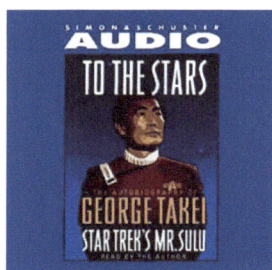

Takei is campaigning for a new *Star Trek* television series staring Captain Sulu. "My goal is to continue, on a regular basis, share Captain

Sulu's heroism and dash and romance with the audience on a weekly basis." A step in the right direction is the original Captain Sulu adventures released by Simon & Schuster Audio. The second in the series, *Cacophony* by Peter David, will be available in October. Many fans have written to Paramount voicing their support for more Captain Sulu adventures. Takei is very aware of the strength the fans have to shape Star Trek and encourages all fans to write to Paramount.

To The Stars is a written with style, grace and humour. From the internment during World War II to seeing the Paramount gates for the first time. From his first acting job—doing voice overs for the classic SF movie Rodan with Keye Luke to meeting Gene Roddenberry for the first time. From stabbing Jimmy Dohan with a sword (it was Jimmy's fault!) to sitting in the captain's chair aboard the Excelsior to conducting salary negotiations with Paramount, Takei's life is a fascinating and sometimes horrifying look at the American political system and Hollywood—which have surprising similarities.

First published in the Star Trek Communicator.

TERRY BROOKS

by Salman A. Nensi

Terry Brooks was a small town lawyer for 17 years. *He had always wanted to be a writer but knew that it was practically impossible to make a living and raise a family on what you make as a writer. So, he studied law and began to practice while writing in the evening. With over ten books and three million copies in print, Terry Brooks is one of the most successful fantasy writers of our time. The* Tangle Box, *the fourth book in the Magic Kingdom series will be published in hardcover this April by Del Rey Books.*

S: Let's talk about being a lawyer—it was a long time ago...

T: What a scary thought. It was a long time ago and I've almost blotted it from my memory.

S: Try and think back.

T: I was in a small town practice—a five member firm of general practitioners. We took whatever walked through the door on any given day. You pretty much got to see the beginning and end of things and I liked that aspect of practicing law quite a bit. There was not so much delayed gratification and you really could work with people on a one to one basis, and usually do some good for them. I did it for 17 years and for most of that 17 years I enjoyed it. Towards the end I started to have a conflict between the writing and the practice, which hurt my enthusiasm for the law somewhat because I was always going to be a writer first and foremost. Also there were quite a few changes in the nature of practicing law that bothered me. It became a great deal more paperwork and there was an awful lot of new legislation. It became difficult to do a general practitioner's work.

S: You were a lawyer, now you're a successful writer. John Grisham was also a lawyer as was William Deverall... is there something about being a lawyer that gives one an insight into the human condition that aids in writing?

T: I think you could make that argument. Certainly you work with people who are under a lot of stress and who are dealing with very real and difficult problems. I think, you tend to see the best and the worst of people in those conditions and that's a good thing for a writer. It is inspirational in a lot of ways, I think, because of that. I don't think it is a particularly good profession for the mechanics of writing, however. Legal writing tends to be extremely stilted and not very innovative. That's not particularly good for a writer of fiction to become immersed in. You could argue that the one balances the other out. I used to make that argument all the time to keep my sanity. I would practice law and I would be in the real world and I could go home and write fantasy and get away from all that. I'd take from a little bit of one into the other. Then there was the other argument. I used to go to talks and people would say, 'how come a lawyer writes fantasys, isn't that different' and I'd say, well no, very much the same.

Both professions involve people who are wordsmiths. If you are a trial lawyer, for example, which I was, and I think Grisham was and Scott Turrow and maybe Deverall too... If words are your tools I think you certainly can see the way that would carry over to being a writer. Much of being a lawyer is putting together the puzzle, of working thoughts and concepts and logic through and reasoning out ideas. There is a lot that carries over between the two professions.

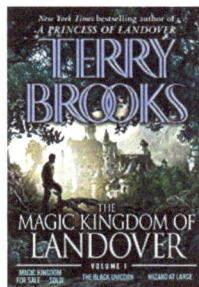

S: Let's jump ahead a little. You finished your first Shannara book and sent it off to Del Rey. Somebody picked up the phone and called you and you were a star.

T: Not exactly. It was a little more complex than that. I actually submitted it the first time to Daw Publishing. Don Walheim had it 6 or 8 months. We exchanged a couple of letters. He was interested but he sent it back at the end and said it was too big and too risky but he liked the story and thought it would find a home and why didn't I send it to Judy Lynn Del Rey over at Ballantine books who had just come in as science fiction editor. Of course I did, along with Don Walheim's letter and it got there just as she was making a pitch to have Lester, her husband, hired as fantasy editor. When the book came in she took a look at it (I found all this out years later, I didn't know any of it at the time) and she said 800 pages, what do I know, Lester look at this see if it is worth anything. Lester got hold of it and he liked it so much that when he went into accept the job he said he'd take the job if they'd let him publish this as his first book, under the Del Rey imprint. They agreed. Then Lester wrote me a letter. He did an interesting thing. In his first paragraph he said this is potentially the best work of fantasy since Tolken's Lord of the Rings. That was the carrot. Then for the next four of five paragraphs he described the amount of work that I was going to have to do in order to make it an acceptable piece of fiction. That was just the beginning. He was a very tough, hard editor, but that was the beginning and it was very exciting to an unpublished, no nothing writer from the midwest.

S: They still look through the slush pile at Del Rey...

T: Oh yeah, they do. They do it at a number of publishing houses, but they have a real commitment to it at Del Rey. I go up there all the time and they've still got stacks and stacks of unpublished manuscripts sitting around. They go through them and occasionally they will find somebody. They still publish the Del Rey Discovery series as part of their program to promote new authors, authors they feel haven't gotten significant recognition and need a little extra push.

S: With your first book Lester gave you a lot of direction.

T: Yes, he helped with every book I wrote, less so in the latter years for various reasons. Hopefully because I had learned some lessons.

S: I have a copy of the manuscript here for *The Tangle Box* and there are very few editing marks on it at all.

T: Well you know I have been lucky enough, he says knocking on wood, not to have had a significant rewrite on any book since *Wishsong*. That is about 7 books back.

S: Is that because your talent has been crafted? Is it a question of working out 3 or 4 books and finally getting to that stage where you know what the editor wants before the editor gets it?

T: Some of it is definitely a progressive kind of thing. I was heavily, heavily edited on the first 3 books that I wrote in the Shannara series. I did an extensive rewrite on *Sword*, rewrites that went on for a long period of time. The next book I submitted, which was a Shannara sequel, Lester Del Rey turned down, just flat turned it down. But he also did a page by page analysis of why the book didn't work. I rewrote it for *Elfstones*, submitted *Elfstones* and he made me rewrite the middle 200 pages of *Elfstones* from scratch. I did a huge amount of rewriting in those first couple of books and I learned an awful lot about what it takes to be a nuts & bolts kind of writer. I think a lot of those lessons were learned early on fortunately and certainly they are the kind of lessons you don't forget easily. I have been able to avoid a lot of the pitfalls that you might otherwise fall into and that's been, I think, increasingly true as the books have gone on. You hope you retain some of what you have learned early.

The other thing is that I do all my work by submitting an outline first. The editor looks at what the outline is, sees the story, gets a description of the characters, gets an overview of what the story is supposed to accomplish and what it is going to do because I do both a chapter by chapter and a story synopsis. We talk it out and we go back and forth on it and we hash out most of the potential problems up front and I think that saves an awful lot on rewrites as well.

S: Can you describe the difference between Lester's style and Owen's [Owen Lock, Del Rey's editor-in-chief] style?

T: Oh I think so. Lester was extremely opinionated and had some very hard and fast rules. He had a lifetime's experience behind him when I met him—as a writer in the field of science fiction principally, as a critic and as an editor. He had been around for 40 years in the field when he started with me. Owen's been in the field the same length of time I have which is about 16 to 18 years, as an editor. Owen is a much more easy going personality. He's my contemporary, we kind of grew up in the business together. We are close friends, so ours is more of an equals friendship kind of relationship, whereas Lester was always more of a father figure. I was much more careful about crossing Lester. I held him in a great deal of awe and the relationship was considerably different because of where we had both come from. That relationship changed things completely. Both ways work and I was fortunate that I had Lester early on because I probably needed that kind of an editor in the beginning–somebody who you wouldn't question. If he says it's so it's so and you would just do it because he had the experience and I didn't. Now after having had that exposure I think it is better for me to have somebody like Owen that I am more comfortable working with. We exchange ideas and we talk back and forth and neither of us pulls any punches and I think that kind of helps.

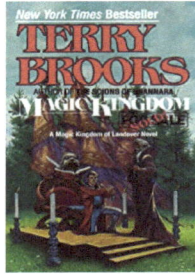

S: *The Sword of Shannara* was the first fiction book to hit the *New York Times* Trade Paperback bestseller list. Two very successful Shannara books followed that. All of a sudden, *Magic Kingdom*. Where did the impetus for something different come from?

T: Well, it was a combination of things. After I wrote *Wishsong* I had at that point more than 10 years of writing Shannara books and I was fed up to the teeth with them. I really couldn't do another one and do it justice. I told Lester that I had to write something else and he said well you should anyway and this is as good a time as any. I asked him if he had any ideas. I said I wanted to write something that is shorter. Something that is related in some way to to the contemporary world and that has more humor to it. He said, I do have an idea but I don't think you are the right writer for it. Finally I beat him down and he told me what the idea was and it was the skeleton of the *Magic Kingdom* book. Lester said he'd give me the idea for a year and if I developed it and wrote it it'd be mine. Otherwise I'd have to give it back. I took it home and worked it over but he had envisioned it as being sort of a Piers Anthony *Xanth* kind of story. I'm not really built to do anything that involves puns and that much humor in a book, that was too much for me, I'm always looking for the dark side of it. So I said, well what can I do with this, what's this book about? It was about a lawyer, who gave up his practice, bought this magic kingdom and then found out it wasn't all what it was cracked up to be but it was still a challenge that was significant enough that he wanted to stay with it. I decided what this book was really about was my transition from becoming a lawyer to becoming a writer. So I used that as the metaphorical underpinnings of the book and sat down to figure out how it could be developed after that. That started the whole philosophy of the idea of Ben Holiday on the one hand as King and the power of his alter ego on the other.

S: Who then is your alter ego if you are Ben Holliday?

T: Well I have both of those sides in me. I have both the creator and the destroyer sides. I guess as a writer and you are always warring them with the two, I think, in some ways because there is a certain self-destructive bent to anyone who wants to be a writer anyway. (laughter)

S: (laughter) Do you want to explain that?

T: (laughter) Well, it is just that you are really setting yourself up to be knocked down every time you try to do something. You are going to have critics. You are going to be your own worst critic. You are going to always question whether you did the best job you could. You'd savage an awful lot of what you do and do it again and do it again. You have a lot of dark thoughts about what you are doing and whether it is the right thing. You are dealing with a lot of issues that reflect, I do anyway, issues that reflect what's going on in the real world. So you spend a lot of time dwelling on that and it can be self-destructive.

S: Here's a little aside how do you feel about the town you grew up in, Sterling, Illinois?

T: It's a good place to be from.

S: Sterling Silver, the castle, is a very nurturing place.

T: Yeah, it responds very well to the King...

S: It keeps him safe. Have you been back to Sterling?

T: The Sterling that I grew up in doesn't exist anymore for all intents and purposes. I've been back there. I go back because my parents still live there, so I go back once in a while. It holds a lot of fond memories and it was a good place to be growing up in when I was a boy, but it is not the same anymore. It has undergone terrific economic changes. It's economic base of support has changed considerably. A lot of it has been bulldozed back into the earth, so it has changed quite a bit.

S: I want to talk a little bit about the destructive side of being a write. How does that side of you deal with the tremendous amount of praise that your books have received?

T: Oh I don't know, I don't tend to take most of that seriously. (laughter).

S: How can you not? Here's some quotes: "Brooks keep's the story going at full gallop." "A wonderfully heartstopping series..."

T: I think people are paid to say those things.

S: Reviewers are paid to say these things about books, but which books they say them about is up to them.

T: I am a writer who writes to be read first and foremost. I am a commercial fiction writer so I like the idea that people buy these books and read them. I don't spend much time worrying about their critical acclaim. I want people to read my books and I want them to come away saying 'Wow that's a great book.' That's very important. I try to focus on that part of it and I do appreciate the letters I get from people who are not paid reviewers but who have read a book and the book has really made some kind of a difference to them because that's what effected me growing up and still affects me as a reader. I would still like to find a book that just knocks my socks off. Somebody who really speaks to the things that concern me and will write the kind of story that makes me think wow I wish I could have written that story.

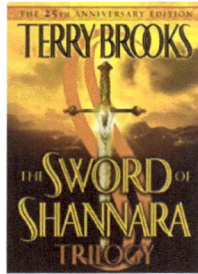

S: Do you respond to mail from your readers?

T: Oh always, I always write back.

S: So we should encourage people to write to you c/o of Del Rey Books.

T: It takes a while sometimes for me to get back to them. It can take 30 to 60 days, depending on where I am and how long it takes the mail to get to me. But I answer all my own mail still.

S: In a recent People Magazine article the writer has quoted you as saying that you are just a little peeved that you are not a media darling.

T: (laughter) yeah, those People people!

S: And the article goes on to quote, "If I could just get the kind of courage that John Grisham gets."

T: Yeah, don't we all wish that?

S: Well, I don't know... Do you really wish that?

T: Well, I do. The commercial side of me wishes it. The rational human being side of me says, what, are you nuts. I still like the idea I can go almost anywhere and not be recognized and that's good. I lead a normal life. On the other hand I am always looking for a way to get other people to try the books and find new readers. You reach a certain point where it is really hard to do if you don't get some kind of media support.

S: So you're a self-admitted commercial writer. You said in the *People* magazine article, and I quote, "I kind of like the fact that my characters exist in people's imaginations and I wonder if my books would lose something by putting them on the screen." After the success of *Jurassic Park, Rising Sun, The Firm* and *Pelican Brief*, do you still feel that way?

T: That's a good question. I've been asking myself that very question lately. On the one hand I'm concerned that if I sold the movie rights that they would destroy the story in some way. Once you sell it you don't own it anymore and the movie people are going to do what they are going to do with it. On the other hand there is no denying the marketing effect that making a movie of a writer's books have and we can talk about Michael Crichton, John Grisham and now Anne Rice with *Interview With The Vampire*. Certainly if you can get a movie made it opens a lot of potential doors for book sales that you couldn't reach otherwise. There's a whole other crowd out there that's difficult in reaching in the absence of having that movie made. It's a tradeoff of one to the other. Grisham said a good thing one time in an interview he did where they asked that very question. They asked him what control did he have and he said, 'I look at it this way. When I sold the movie rights I didn't ask to have any control. They made the movie. If it's a good movie it's to their credit. On the other hand they don't take credit for what I do on my books.' Maybe that's the way to look at it.

S: After selling four *New York Times* bestsellers to the movie industry I'm sure he has a little more control than he did.

T: Who has ever done that? I mean his track record–there isn't anybody else out there. This has been an interesting couple of years of firsts with what Grisham did with 4 of his 5 books that are in print and what Robert Waller has done with the *Bridges of Madison County* and now *Slow Waltz at Ceader Creak*.

S: We spent an interesting Summer watching the Best-seller list, counting the number of Grisham titles verses the number of Crichton titles.

T: Crichton is the the one who interests me because the selling of *Jurassic Park* brought all of his old books back on the Best Seller list. What a feat that is. It's a great thing for Ballantine to have accomplished and a terrific thing for the author. There are a lot of ways that you can parlay that kind of thing into sales and it would be a great thing to do.

But, you know it is a little hard to gripe. I've had such great success overall. I feel a little weird sitting here saying, well, but I want more, more, more.

S: I understood that you had sold the movie rights to *The Sword*.

T: Early on but I got it back fortunately. That was the thing that really set me off on this question because the people who bought the rights redid the storyline and made it into a piece of science fiction with genetic mutation and computers. It was really scary. They completely altered the story and after that I was very gun shy about going back to the movie people.

S: With the release of Jurassic Park, not to beat a dead dinosaur to death, there seems to be renewed interest in science fiction, fantasy and speculative fiction. I have a few stats here: 52 million people watch science fiction programming weekly, 11 million bought a science fiction book in the past 12 months, 8 million people in the U.S. have rented a science fiction video in the last month. With numbers like this, why then do you also see a categorization of science fiction? Why do you think Jurassic Park came out as fiction rather than science fiction?

T: Well I think that science fiction and fantasy have always been considered to be a category fiction. If you have something come out of that field that is successful like *Jurassic Park* then it is not science fiction anymore.

S: It is!

T: No, it is something else. There has always been that kind of transformation. Well we have science fiction and then we have so on and so forth. There has always been that makeover. Fantasy, for example, outsells science fiction something two or three to one on the book field it is quite a bit stronger. I don't know what to say about that except there is certainly a reticence on the part of the reading public in general and the movie going public in particular to read either fantasy or science fiction unless there is some particular author that they like or a particular book that catches their fancy. I would certainly say Jurassic Park was one of those. It was a great idea.

Originally published in Cryptych Magazine.

NENSI.COM

PUBLISHING & AGENTING

Trumplethinskin and Tiny Hands Press | The Bakka Book
Collection | StoneFox Publishing | Fall of Ancients |
Fire Hornet Codex | TEGG, Inc. | Agenting

> "Indefatigable."
> **ELAINE CUNNINGHAM**
> Author

"Sal's level of initiative is spectacular, often bordering on the astounding."
—Judith and Garfield Reeves-Stevens
(New York Times best-selling novelists)

1992 to present

Since 1992, Nensi has been a pioneer in the Canadian publishing industry. In 2020 he published The Tales of Trumplethinskin; a trilogy of Children's Books for Adults. Nensi's many accomplishments include:

- travelling across China and selling new titles to Chinese publishers and government ministries (the first Canadian to do so in years), as well as lecturing about Western media and intellectual property rights;
- reuniting former employees of Toronto's Bakka Books who had gone on to become professional writers to publish The Bakka Anthology; and,
- founding an imprint (Bakka Books), which continues to issue science-fiction titles to the current day.

Some author-clients include: Celine Dion, Dave Duncan, Canadian Broadcasting Corporation (productions of Oscar Wilde's plays), Cory Doctorow, Robert J. Sawyer, Spider Robinson, Ed Greenwood, and Phyllis Gotlieb.

Over the years, Nensi has connected a vibrant community of writers and publishers. His gift for finding the right people to make things happen has helped him expand the reach and success of Canadian publishing and many Canadian authors.

PUBLISHER/CO-PUBLISHER/BOOK DESIGNER, BOOK WORKS

Trumplethinskin

"Trumplethinskin: Donald Trump in a nutshell."

URBAN DICTIONARY

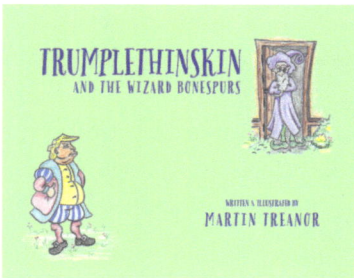

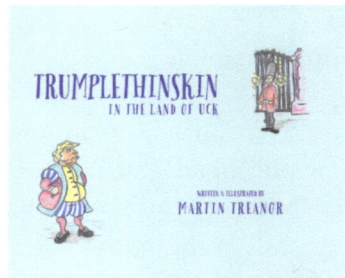

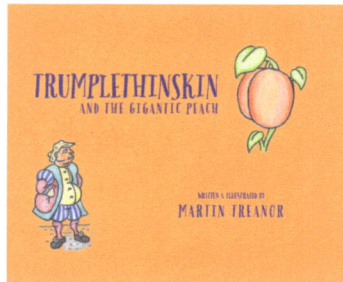

- 3 books, 3 adventures, 3 levels of narcissistic idiocy
- Satirical, politically charged storybooks for adults | 32 A4 landscape pages per book | English | ebook, POD, audio, gift and omnibus editions.
- Illustrated and authored by Martin Treanor
- English, German, and Arabic as ebooks, POD paperbacks and hardcovers with merchandise, games and a hardcover collector's gift edition omnibus.

Published titles:

Trumplethinskin and the Wizard Bonespurs:

Trumplethinskin discovers he will be sent to a nasty place called Vet Nam, and devises ways to avoid going, visiting the Wizard Bonespurs—who can make-believe anything.

Trumplethinskin in the Land of UcK:

Trumplethinskin travels to the Land of UcK, where he is brought to the palace for an afternoon tea and realizes all he really wants is his own throne room. So, he instructs his elf Pomelo to get him one, along with the Land of UcK and the Isle of Green at the top of the world.

Trumplethinskin and the Gigantic Peach:

Dancy Nancy is growing a Gigantic Peach for Trumplethinskin, who detests fruit. He needs Chucky Dollson, Tight-fisted Turtle, and Hennity Bennity to help him, because he has promised them bagfuls of magic beans.

For more please visit:

- TheTalesOfTrumplethinskin.com
- MartinTreanor.com
- ANiceCuppaTea.com
- IPHabitat-TheTalesOfTrumplethinskin.info

Tiny Hands Press

"I'm willing to believe that there might be a few people who don't have a 'used car salesman within.' I can think of some people who don't. There's Mother Teresa for one. And there was a kid in my fourth grade class who used to eat dirt, or anything he could find. He probably didn't have a used car salesman within either. But the rest of us certainly do. We need it to tell the white lies we need to survive: to call in sick, fill out our tax forms, and to say to the person lying next to you 'I love you.'"

STEVE BOWDEN
Author

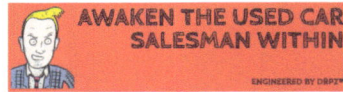

Awaken the Used Car Salesman Within

Lying. Everybody lies. Big lies, little lies, white lies and lies wholly designed to serve our self–interest. It is a subject we are all familiar with, and are all prepared to laugh at. Seinfeld's George Costanza is funny because he lies constantly, not because he tells the truth. Bad behavior makes for great humor. Used Car Salesmen are guilty of the worst behavior of all and the entire nation knows it.

For more please visit:
- AwakenTheUsedCarSalesmanWithin.com
- TPSBowden.com
- TBigZebra.com

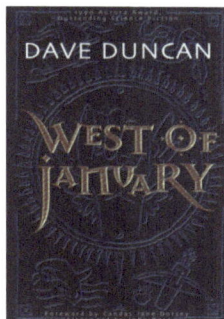

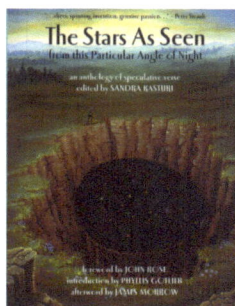

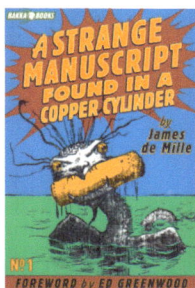

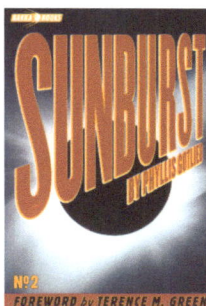

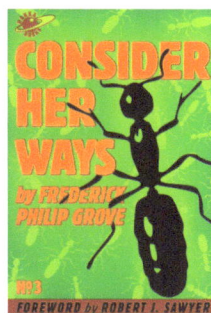

The Bakka Book Collection

"A Strange Manuscript Found in a Copper Cylinder has been much admired as a Swiftian satire."

BIOGRAPHI.CA

The Bakka Book Collection

- *West of January* by Dave Duncan, Red Deer Press, 2002
- *The Bakka Anthology* edited by John Rose, Bakka Books, 2002
- *The Stars as Seen From This Particular Angle of the Night* edited b Sandra Kasturi, Red Deer Press, 2003
- *A Strange Manuscript Found in a Copper Cylinder* by James De Mille, StoneFox Publishing, 2001
- *Sunburst* by Phyllis Gotlieb, StoneFox Publishing, 2001
- *Consider Her Ways* by Fredrick Philip Grove, StoneFox Publishing, 2001

The StoneFox Collection

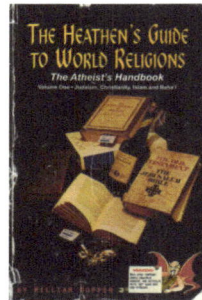

The StoneFox Collection

- *The Parent's Guide to Street Drugs* by James M. Lange, StoneFox Publishing, 2001
- *The Heathen's Guide to World Religions* by William Hopper, StoneFox Publishing, 2001

Fire Hornet Codex

"In the midst of chaos . . ."

SUN TZU

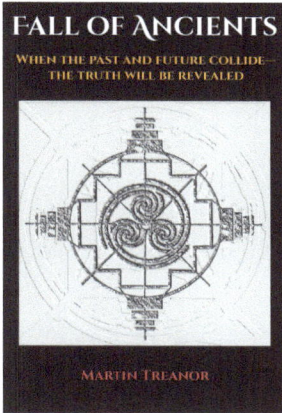

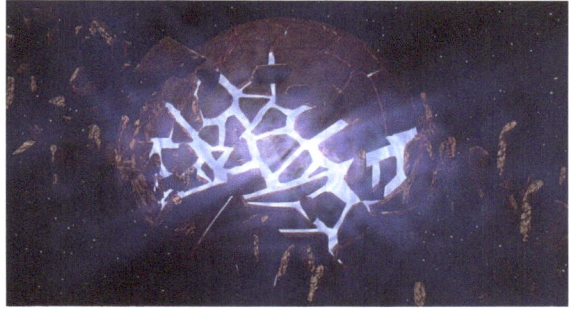

Fall of Ancients

A four-part, multimedia, fictional entertainment package spanning thousands of years of world history from the Last Glacial Maximum (LGM) —circa 26,500BP—through the modern era, and onward to a proposed future with universal consequences.

- *Deceit of Ages*
- *Arcadia's End*
- *Destruction Seed*
- *The Legends of Loon Creek*

For more please visit:
- FallOfAncients.com
- FireHornetCodex.com
- IPHabitat-FallOfAncients.info
- MartinTreanor.com
- ANiceCuppaTea.com

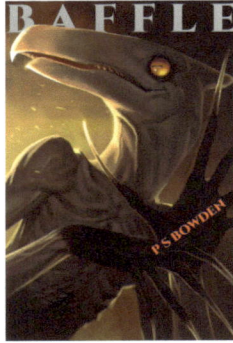

Baffle

The Demon shied from one to another, to maintain comfort in his human form. He had seen humans do this plenty of times, and decided that this was socially acceptable.

He was enjoying his morning coffee while out at a greasy spoon he favoured.

He liked the place as it served food he enjoyed . . . but the humans?

He did not care for them.

For more please visit:
  • FireHornetCodex.com
  • PSBowden.com
  • BigZebra.com

TEGG, Inc.

The Greenwood Collection

- *The Path Less Traveled*
- *Grandpa's Best Christmas Ever*
- *All is Lust*
- A Platter of Surprises Collections
    - *A Miscellany of Luxating Palinodes: Platter of Surprises Vol 3.*
        - ► *The Day The Aliens Landed*
        - ► *Ravilantar*
        - ► *The Butler Did It*
        - ► *Not A Lot of Trust*
        - ► *Hosting the Holy One*
    - *A Congress of Delightful Naughtiness: Platter of Surprises Vol. 2*
        - ► *The Duchess Defenestrates*
        - ► *Wild She Was, and Golden-Eyed*
        - ► *Dragonback Sex*
        - ► *To Ride a Maiden Knight*
        - ► *The Queen's Forbidden Garden*
    - *A Modest Gallimaufry of Brief Tales: Platter of Surprises Vol. 1*
        - ► *The Ostrond File*
        - ► *A Nice Silky Merlot*
        - ► *The Wizard Who Was Everywhere*
        - ► *Walking the King's Skull*
        - ► *The King's Very Long Day*

The Hellmaw Collection

- *Your World is Doomed* by Ed Greenwood
- *Dragon Dreams* by Chris A. Jackson
- *Blind Justice* by Erik Scott de Bie
- *Soul Larcenist* by Suzanne Church
- *Eye of Glass* by Marie Bilodeau
- *Incubus Tweets* by J. Robert King
- *Of the Essence* by Gabrielle Harbowy
- *My Talons in Her Throat* by Ed Greenwood
- *Honeyboy's Hunt* by Marie Bilodeau
- *Stormbringer* by Steve Bornstein
- *Throckmorton's Trick* by Ed Greenwood
- *The Mark of Five* by Txabier Etxeberri Otxoa
- *Baffle* by P. Steve Bowden
- *The Fishing Hole* by Richard Lee Byers
- *Into History* by Steve Bornstein
- *Suicidal Saviour* by J. Robert King
- *Dark Creed* by Martin Treanor
- *Small World* by Gabrielle Harbowy

The Stormtalons Collection

- *Words of Unbinding* by Ed Greenwood
- *Grayshade* by Gregory A. Wilson
- *The Pirate King's Daughter* by Dileep S. Rangan
- *The Ghost in the Stone* by Richard Lee Byers
- *The Queen's Scourge* by Chris A. Jackson
- *Not As They Appear* by C. J. Jarrett
- *Flesh and Artifice* by Jaleigh Johnson
- *Words of Unbinding* by Ed Greenwood
- *A Scourge in Hand* by Chris A. Jackson
- *The Ghost in the Stone* by Richard Lee Byers
- *Before They Appeared* by C. J. Jarrett
- *Wizard Sitting* by Brandon Crilly
- *An Act of Faith* by Sarah Ceiliann
- *The Tower of Egizii* by Leslie Donaldson

Folklore: The Affliction Collection

- *The Whispering Skull* by Ed Greenwood
- *Black Alithe* by Nicholas Fife

The Mirt Collection

- *All Things Through The Bright Flames*

The Onder Media Group Collection

- *Onder Magazine*
- *Onder Radio*

Agenting

"This book would never be without you—
so you really do have my eternal gratitude!"

SANDRA KASTURI
Editor of *The Stars as Seen* (Red Deer Press)

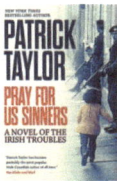

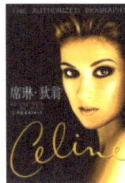

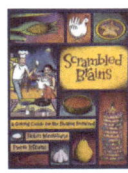

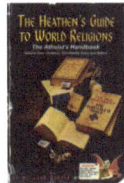

Agented Books

- *Pray for Us Sinners* by Patrick Taylor
- *Awaken The Used Car Salesman Within* by P. Steve Bowden
- *Céline Dion biography*—Chinese rights
- *Reel Vancouver* by Ken MacIntyre
- *Remember That Christmas*—Canadian rights
- *Scrambled Brains* by Robin Konstabaris
- *The Heathen's Guide to World Religions* by William Hopper

PRODUCER | DEVELOPER | LECTURER | EVENT ARCHITECT

Audioworks | Film Work | Event Architect | Lectures | Appointments

AUDIOWORKS

"Oh gee, I just noticed the attachment at the end of this email.
You are an incomparable planner!"

ANDREW TAY
Audiographer

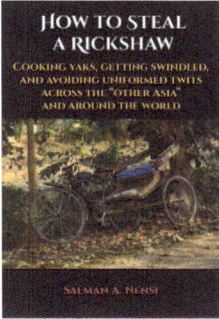

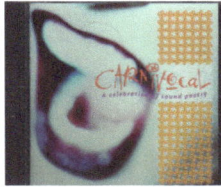

- *How to Steal a Rickshaw*, an episodic audiobook, Zariqa.com, 2021
- *Carnivocal a celebration of sound poetry*, Red Deer Press, 1999
- *Mother Teresa a tribute*, coordinator Jim Briggs, 2000
- *Salome by Oscar Wilde*, Canadian Broadcasting Corporation / StoneFox Publishing, 2000
- *The Importance of Being Earnest* by Oscar Wilde, Canadian Broadcasting Corporation / StoneFox Publishing, 2000
- *Book Bits Sampler, interviews by Craig Rintoul*, BookBits, 2001
- *Onder Radio*, The Ed Greenwood Group, 2016
- *Shanger One: The Alison Project*, private labeled CD (Toronto / New Zealand)
- *Shanger Two: The Seoul Project*, private labeled CD (Seoul, South Korea)

FILM WORK

"I can see how hard you're working and I appreciate you're doing
all you can to ensure a smooth operation of this . . ."

"I just wanna say thanks again for everything, it's been a pleasure to meet
and work with you both. You've both been true gents, and I hope we get to
work together again sometime in the future."

MAX AARON PALMER
Videographer

Film-related Works

- Sex and Death Short Film Fest: marketing, development, logistics
- Reel Asian Film Fest: development and fundraising
- Bell and Bell ExpressVu: production assistant and set decoration
- Independent production assistant, set decoration, fundraising,
logistics, sales and craft services for film (fiction and documentary)
producers (Toronto, Vancouver, Seoul, Kabul, Bangkok, Siem Reap.)

EVENT ARCHITECT

"I would like to personally thank you for the outstanding job you did at
CBA. I never had so many favourable comments on our booth,
books and people."

MARK STANTON
President, Raincoast Books

- TEGG Annual Conclave; 21 days straight, 18 high profile guests . . .
only 2 spare bedrooms!
- Annual Robbie Burns parties
- Canadian Booksellers Association annual convention closing party
- "Sex & Money" Canadian Lesbian and Gay Archive fundraiser
- Brant Street Club Christmas party
- Sex and Death Short Film Festival fundraisers (baccanals)
- PEN Canada annual benefit

- Ghandavar Creations (private adult-themed parties logistics)
- Private Wine and Scotch Tastings (with culinary pairings and sales)
- Harvest Festival (Ontario, Canada) volunteer
- Themed gatherings from 5 to 400 such as Iron Chef nights, wine and the most intriguing cheese you can find, costumes, treasure hunts and city explorations.

PUBLIC APPEARANCES, LECTURES, TALKS AND PRESENTATIONS

"While many people are reasonable planners, very few have the energy and drive necessary to consistently put complex plans into motion and see each step executed flawlessly. Mr. Nensi's creative energy has been a huge asset to my company and I unhesitatingly give him my strongest endorsement."

ALEX KAMMER
Producer, Gamehole Con

Topics: media relations, business presentations, publishing technology, book publishing, electronic books, marketing principles and methods
- Seoul National University, Seoul, South Korea (http://www.useoul.edu)
- American University, Bishkek, Kyrgyzstan (http://www.auca.kg)
- Chinese Book Publishers Association, Beijing, China
- Association of Canadian Publishers, Toronto, Canada (http://publishers.ca)
- Paramount Pictures Events, Toronto, Canada (http://www.paramount.com)
- New York Toy Fair, New York, USA (http://www.toyassociation.org)
- Organization of Book Publishers of Ontario, Toronto, Canada (http://www.obpo.ca)
- West Coast Publishers Association, Vancouver, Canada
- Tri-Province Publishers Association, Winnipeg, Canada

JUDGING/PANELS/MODERATING

*"Thanks for all your hard work on our behalf.
It's been a real pleasure to work with you!"*

DIANE TEIGISER
Director, Licensing and Merchandising, Playmate Toys Inc.

Publishing:
- Book Publishing Professionals Association
- Book Promoters' Association of Canada
- Simon Fraser University Masters of Publishing program
participation's final projects (Vancouver, 1995)

Star Trek:
- New York radio costume surprise contest judge (New York Toy Fair)
- City of Toronto Star Trek Anniversary Convention; contest judge

Arirang TV talk show appearance (Seoul, South Korea, 2009)

BOARD APPOINTMENTS
AND OTHER ENGAGEMENTS

*"You are a true professional and a BPPA superstar.
'Infinite Thanks' for helping out at the last minute."*

**BOOK PUBLISHING PROFESSIONALS' ASSOCIATION,
JANUARY 2001**

- Board Member and Publications Manager, Canadian & Lesbian Gay
Archives, (2002~2004)
- President (2000~2002), Executive Member (1994~2002), Book
Promoters Association of Canada
- Member (1998~2002), Panel Moderator (2000~2002), Book Publishing
Professionals Association
- Member, Canadian Public Relations Society, (1995~1998)
- Affiliate Member, Science Fiction and Fantasy Writers Association,
(1993~1998)
- Co-founder and Chair, York University's Mass Communication
Student Federation, (1990~1991)

NENSI.COM

TESTIMONIALS

Executive | Clients | Colleagues | Authors/Creators |
Storytelling, Writing & Creativity

EXECUTIVE

"Sal is a very bright light."
~David Kent, president Random House Canada

Salman's strengths? "People skills. Commitment to taking a job through
to completion. Attitude—no complaints, no excuses.
Creativity and inventiveness."
~Judith and Garfield Reeves-Stevens,
author of numerous NYTimes Bestsellers

"Sal has a fantastic, almost anarchic, approach to marketing. His first
instinct is to say "why not" rather than "why."
He works very hard, especially when enthused."
~Kevin Chapman, vice president sales and marketing, General Publishing

"Inspired It's the perfect patron engagement plan."
~Dave Robison, vice president The Ed Greenwood Group

"Probably the most organized and efficient
publicity operation I have ever seen."
~Robert Mackwood, North by Northwest Communications

"...organized, creative, independent and thorough."
~Susan Renouf, editorial director, Doubleday Book Clubs

"Sal is extremely well organized with good ideas for increasing sales
productivity. He is an asset to this company."
~Connie Penn, manager Classic Bookshops

"My sincerest thanks for your dedication and good humour
over these difficult months..."
~Wendy Setterington, area manager, Classic Bookshops

"His attention to detail, accuracy and speed make him
a very reliable and diligent worker."
~Stephan Bucher, president, Doubleday Book Clubs

"I would like to personally thank you for the outstanding job you did at CBA. I never had so many favourable comments on our booth, books and people."
~Mark Stanton, president, Raincoast Books

"Publicity department stacks up against, and in many cases exceeds, the quality I see in other publishing houses."
~Robert Mackwood, North by Northwest Communications

"You really are invaluable to us all. I mean that."
~Ed Greenwood, president, The Ed Greenwood Group

"Your brain is operating on a level most mortals don't grok. Some people MULTI-task... you SIMUL-task. It's a beautiful thing."
~Dave Robison, vice president The Ed Greenwood Group

"... in the short time he has been here, he has had substantial impact on the marketing processes in the division."
~Kevin Chapman, vice president sales and marketing, General Publishing

"You're supposed to be having a day off!
Aren't you missing the point somewhat?"
~Kevin Chapman, vice president sales and marketing, General Publishing

"Understepping, overstepping ... it's great, keep it going."
~Kevin Chapman, vice president sales and marketing, General Publishing

"Considering you had no time to set this up, and we all know what a joy Bruce is to work with, this is an impressive list."
~Kevin Chapman, vice president sales and marketing, General Publishing

"[Salman] has had a substantial impact on the marketing processes in the division."
~Kevin Chapman, vice president sales and marketing, General Publishing

"[Salman] makes other people look dull in ideas terms."
~Kevin Chapman, vice president sales and marketing, General Publishing

"Sal is at his best when put under pressure."
~Kevin Chapman, vice president sales and marketing, General Publishing

[Salman's] level of initiative is? "Seriously high."
~Kevin Chapman, vice president sales and marketing, General Publishing

"Very, very creative and committed. Has wide range of business skills.
Enthuses those around him."
~Kevin Chapman, vice president sales and marketing, General Publishing

Salman is "Very good with peers."
~Kevin Chapman, vice president sales and marketing, General Publishing

"Sal is one of those people who can be hard to hold down in management
terms but delivers so much it is easily worth while.
He has been a boon both times I hired him."
~Kevin Chapman, vice president sales and marketing, General Publishing

"We have been impressed by Sal's diligence, attention to detail, accuracy,
and the speed with which he carried out our requests."
~Judith and Garfield Reeves-Stevens,
author of numerous NYTimes Bestsellers

"Sal is, and always has been, a pleasure to work with."
~Judith and Garfield Reeves-Stevens,
author of numerous NYTimes Bestsellers

"Sal's enthusiasm for and dedication to the
project at hand is always reassuring."
~Judith and Garfield Reeves-Stevens,
author of numerous NYTimes Bestsellers

"[Salman's] ability to maintain a sense of humour while dealing with
unexpected changes in plans and deadlines is greatly appreciated. Sal has
always successfully completed every assignment he's undertaken for us,
often with results that have exceeded the original goals we've set."
~Judith and Garfield Reeves-Stevens,
author of numerous NYTimes Bestsellers

"In our experience, it is rare to find someone who
possesses both Sal's skills and positive attitude."
~Judith and Garfield Reeves-Stevens,
author of numerous NYTimes Bestsellers

"Sal has a great ability to take an "amorphous" project, such as planning a publicity campaign, and setting out concrete, written proposals and schedules."
~Judith and Garfield Reeves-Stevens,
author of numerous NYTimes Bestsellers

"Though we consider ourselves computer-literate and have written and sold computer programs in the past, we have come to depend on Sal's cutting-edge knowledge of trends in electronic media, an area which has growing importance to us as writers."
~Judith and Garfield Reeves-Stevens,
author of numerous NYTimes Bestsellers

"We can always count on Sal to come through for us with quality results and a positive attitude. He probably wouldn't like us to say so, but tight deadlines and impossible challenges seem to invigorate him."
~Judith and Garfield Reeves-Stevens,
author of numerous NYTimes Bestsellers

Salman's level of initiative? "Spectacular, often bordering on the astounding. Sal is always inventive and creative, freeing us from having to micromanage his assignments."
~Judith and Garfield Reeves-Stevens,
author of numerous NYTimes Bestsellers

Salman's limitations? "We haven't found any yet. We know that Sal sometimes becomes frustrated when he's required to work with people who don't keep up with his pace, but we've never seen that frustration affect his work or interfere with a project."
~Judith and Garfield Reeves-Stevens,
author of numerous NYTimes Bestsellers

"[Salman's] attitude is exemplary. He refuses to promise what he cannot deliver but when he makes a promise, he keeps it to the letter. He also understands the feelings and concerns of his clients and responds to these sympathetically and professionally."
~Patrick Taylor, author of *An Irish Country Doctor*,
An Irish Country Christmas and *Pray for Us Sinners*

"[Salman] works tirelessly on behalf of his clients."
~Patrick Taylor, author of *An Irish Country Doctor*,
An Irish Country Christmas and *Pray for Us Sinners*

"[Salman] is diplomatic yet firm and tenacious when he
feels his client's interests are at stake."
~Patrick Taylor, author of *An Irish Country Doctor*,
An Irish Country Christmas and *Pray for Us Sinners*

"Nothing rattled this man. He works into the small hours and in my
experience has never missed a deadline."
~Patrick Taylor, author of *An Irish Country Doctor*,
An Irish Country Christmas and *Pray for Us Sinners*

Salman's strengths? "Honesty. Sense of humour. Realism. Reliability.
A great man to have in your corner."
~Patrick Taylor, author of *An Irish Country Doctor*,
An Irish Country Christmas and *Pray for Us Sinners*

Salman's limitations? "None that I could ascertain."
~Patrick Taylor, author of *An Irish Country Doctor*,
An Irish Country Christmas and *Pray for Us Sinners*

"I believe you will look long and hard before you find a better colleague
and I make that remark not as an author beholden to an agent but as a
senior academic who has been involved in hiring and assessing
junior university staff for the last 30 years."
~Patrick Taylor, author of *An Irish Country Doctor*,
An Irish Country Christmas and *Pray for Us Sinners*

CLIENTS

"A giant thank you."
~Ann Ireland, President PEN Canada

"...many of your recommendations will be part of the transition process..."
~Martin Hart-Hansen, UN Nepal Resident Coordinator's office

"Sal brings a great deal of energy, a can-do attitude, creativity, passion and out-of-the-box thinking to projects. He's also fun to work with."
~Michael Kovrig, Senior Adviser,
North East Asiaat International Crisis Group

"Salman's speed sometimes takes your breath away. His globalised team and style of work boost your creativity. They bring you real fun plus high-quality products."
~Thekla Kelbert, UN Country Team coordinator

"When working with Mr. Nensi, it becomes quickly apparent that he possesses an almost instinctive understanding of how audiences engage and interact with ideas."
~David H. Robison, CEO – Corpse Coffee and Tea (Chicago)

"Sal is CRAZY out-of-the box creative, a child of the world with global ideas and perspectives to draw upon."
~Tom Vanek, Vanek Whiskey Events

"It was a fabulous night. Thank you."
~Matt Hughes, President CLGA

"Thank you Sal. I appreciate your amazing energy to want to share the Why with as many people as possible. Very special to have you be a part of this movement. With great appreciation."
~Simon Sinek, author of *Start With Why*

"Thank you Salman, couldn't have done it without your guidance. Please keep them coming as we progress. We share this success with you."
~Nisha Bhimani, Safi Juice (Angola)

"These are not photographs. These are Art."
~Waheed Khan (director, Hewadwal Group)

"Thank you so much for creating this document. I'll make it a working document. The format is perfect."
~Al-Karim Mamani, AKN Industries (South Africa)

"Salman was hired to do a detailed review of the UN Nepal website and provide recommendations as to how it could be improved both from a

design perspective as well as a service provision perspective. He did a very detailed and thorough analysis and provided a wealth of options. He went beyond his terms of reference and put in many more hours and days than agreed since he wanted to make sure we got the full picture.
Highly Recommended."
~Martin Hart-Hansen, CEO and Strategic Planning Advisor
at United Nations Volunteers

"We are a book publishing company, and hired Salman's company to organize publicity around authors touring in support of their books. He was creative and hard-working, and helped us to succeed in our goals to raise the profile of our books and authors."
~Brian Lam, Publisher at Arsenal Pulp Press

"Sal is like a horror film! He absolutely terrifies you at first with his bold, creative approaches to problems. Then he chases you around until you see why you should do what he suggests. Next, he dispatches quickly but efficiently. AND it all works out really well in the end!"
~Craig Rintoul, Producer-Writer-Director at Kushog View Productions

"His abilities ... have created an indelible impression."
~Maya Stepanova (director, Posnayko)

"I'm not sure which was more astonishing, the breadth and creativity of your plan, or the fact that you pulled it off to perfection."
~Gordon Platt (Head, Writing and Publishing Section,
Canada Council for the Arts)

"[Salman's] insights into the strategies and nuances of business communications have been invaluable, allowing us to quickly develop highly effective messaging protocols that leverage
a broad spectrum of platforms."
~David H. Robison, CEO – Corpse Coffee and Tea (Chicago)

"[Salman's] extensive experience across multiple enterprise models provides a comprehensive awareness of how a message can be promulgated and consumed, resulting in actionable strategies that can be adapted to any platform, agenda, or priority."
~David H. Robison, CEO – Corpse Coffee and Tea (Chicago)

"I can, without hesitation, recommend Mr. Nensi to any organization that wishes to create a targeted messaging protocol, streamline its execution and delivery, and be assured of its positive impact."
~David H. Robison, CEO – Corpse Coffee and Tea (Chicago)

"Thanks for all your hard work on our behalf.
It's been a real pleasure to work with you!"
~Diane Teigiser, director of licensing and merchandising,
Playmate Toys Inc.

COLLEAGUES

"Wow!"
~Diana Tigersen, editor

"I unwittingly fell into Salman's orbit and will be forever grateful I did. This is a professional at the top of his game with a breadth of experience Jules Verne couldn't dream up."
~Thomas Dunlop, Navitas North America Student Recruitment Director

"My brain just got injected with mega-ideas, thanks to you. Have not felt like this since about the time I last saw you. You're good for my soul."
~Raj Dash, writer, consultant: apps, film and TV

"You always have the best brain candy. I don't mind at all. I look forward to it."
~Julie Ahern, Greenbrier Games

"We have all been really impressed with the excellence of your product and your service, and yesterday was no exception."
~Felicity Stone, associate editor, Western Living Magazine

"I have thoroughly enjoyed working with Mr. Nensi over the past several years. His organizations skills and professionalism are as good as it gets. While many people are reasonable planners, very few have the energy and drive necessary to consistently put complex plans into motion and see each step executed flawlessly. Mr. Nensi's creative energy has been a huge asset to my company and I unhesitatingly give him my endorsement."
~Alex Kammer, GameHole Con

"You are a true professional and a BPPA superstar."
~Book Publishing Professionals' Association, January 2001

"As soon as began working with Salman, his years of experience in marketing, communications, and planning became obvious. His attention to the minutest detail drew out only the best ideas and concepts, whilst keeping the blood pumping in what (being the creative world) can dead-end with triviality. It is a huge task to organise so many individually creative minds (with all of their idiosyncrasies) and Salman was tireless in keeping us on track, as well as navigating what can be a convoluted and complex business."
~Martin Treanor, author Fall of Ancients (Fire Hornet Codex)

"Thanks for all your hard work on our behalf. It's been a real pleasure to work with you!"
~Diane Teigiser, director of licensing and merchandising, Playmate Toys Inc.

"Sal was instrumental in getting my first article in print. From organising interview subjects and a venue to layout and publication, all went without a hitch."
~David Hart, journalist

"Salman is a detail-oriented manager who maintains excellent client communication and meets deadlines. His work has always exceeded my needs and expectations."
~The Rev. Jonathan Hagey, *Endless Yard Sale Showdown* at Netflix

"Salman is one the most incredibly articulate, well-read, well-rounded and capable marketing professionals I have met in the last few years. His ability to manage, see and respect the most minute of details while consistently observing and pursuing strategic imperatives gives Salman the ability to be a superior leader and excellent mentor. His perennial good nature, strong sense of humour and ability to relate to virtually anyone makes having him a part of the team a true pleasure."
~Bourke Marrison, Bell

"Sal Nensi was a resourceful and highly creative communications specialist, who contributed significantly to the launch and ultimate success of many books published by Simon & Schuster, as well as Alive

Publishing. I highly recommend Sal to anyone interested doing publicity directly or managing a team of individuals who deliver media results."
~Nolan Machan, Effective Online Communicator

"Salman Nensi worked with me when I was Artistic Director of the Vancouver International Writers & Readers Festival. I found him to be creative, innovative and he kept to the timeline. He was also most helpful with his insights into the publishing world that gave me an edge on my colleagues, citing writers who were up and coming and helping with contacts."
~Alma Lee, Arts Consultant, Producer CUFFED Crime Fiction Festival

"Salman was a capable and effective Marketing Manager. With Salman's efforts we were able to achieve a new level of prominence in the marketplace. Salman Nensi was a well-organized employer who gave clear directions with clear expectations. His directions are always perfectly clear, and his projects are impeccably managed."
~Steve Bowden, Writer

"Salman has always been a consummate business professional. My clear memory from 20 plus years ago shows him admirably. Then, a young and upcoming publicist at Random House, Salman invited me to the CN Tower to join he and his out-of-town author for lunch. And a glorious lunch it was: two native Torontonians (Salman and I) regaled the author with hometown tidbits and up-to-date trivia. All the while, Salman, kept a watchful professional eye on simply everything: the food, the drinks, the engagement level of the author—and thankfully, the bill, as well. If you're looking for an effective communicator with smarts, high EQ and a good heart to boot, Salman Nensi is your man."
~Vera N. Held, Columnist, "Make it Work", The Toronto Sun, Careers

"I am grateful to Sal for recognizing my potential as a writer. He also had the uncanny ability to get more work out of me in less time than anyone I've worked for before. In a contract position, you really appreciate someone who forces you to do work that you're later proud of. I'd heartily recommend him for these talents."
~Leo Salloum, Lawyer

"The resume, especially, impressed them so much.
Thank you again for all your help."
~Omar Mahdi, Amazon DSP

"I looked it over, It's great."
~Owen Deveney, cinematographer

"I am really impressed by your courtesy. You are perhaps the nicest person
on earth, who gives suggestions & ideas free of cost."
~Asim Iftikhar, Design Engineer at
KSB Pumps Company Limited – Pakistan

"Oh gee, I just noticed the attachment at the end of this email.
You are an incomparable planner!"
~Andrew Tay, audiographer

"I can see how hard you're working and I appreciate you're doing all you
can to ensure a smooth operation of this ... I just wanna say thanks again
for everything, it's been a pleasure to meet and work with you both.
You've both been true gents, and I hope we get to work together again
sometime in the future :)"
~Max Aaron Palmer, videographer

"So pleased. U r inspirational..."
~Faten Bizzari, City of London

"I have worked with Sal on many projects over a 20 year period and
without reservation I can say that he is the best project manager I have
ever worked with. He is creative, organized and detailed-oriented with a
mind tuned on the bigger picture. He knows how to get the very best out
of his large, international team of professionals. His enthusiasm is
contagious, and he makes you want to perform at your highest level. He
dares to dream big and, if you're lucky, he'll take you along for the ride."
~Patti McCabe, Development, Events and Communications Specialist

"Sal is one of those rare project managers who actually has the skill to
unite a culturally and geographically diverse team to focus on a single
outcome, even when costs and deadlines are constrained. His
international experience has been gained largely from working on-site in

remote locations, giving him a unique understanding of global issues and the various requirements they produce."
~Jon Southurst, Co-Founder at Talon Media Group

"I have known Salman for 30 years. His expertise in the publication business (electronic and hard copy), strategic communications, marketing and business are unparalleled. There is no project too big or too small that cannot benefit from his input. His network of service providers is huge and capable."
~Colin Empke, Experienced Insurance Coverage Counsel

"I have had the great pleasure of working with Salman many times over the last 10 years. He is an exceptional Project Manager able to put to task multiple projects across companies, countries and continents. Always timely and efficient, I have utilized his abilities for a large variety of tasks and projects. Salman is always the first person to mind when looking into new ventures."
~Jason Clark, Compensation Analyst at CIBC Wealth Management

"If I like someone, I like them for who they are and not what they can do for me."
~Marc Coté, publisher

"I'm impressed with your experience and background."
~Brittany Hudson, DSG Consulting

"You're a gem! (I'm serious about your voice!)"
~Rhonda Kerlew, Sum Sanos

"You're a good guy with scruples."
~Mike Grammer, lawyer

"...reliable... pleasant personality and a fine ability to deal tactfully with people."
~Suzanne Cotton, co-worker, Distican

"...extremely capable, hard working and a self starter..."
~Judith Ryde, co-worker, Classic Bookshops

"...dependable with a keen sense of humour..."
~Jean Hutchinson, co-worker, Classic Bookshops

"Nice job on Sources of the River."
~Linda, editor, Sasquatch Books

"Thank you tremendously for all the work you've done on our books,
particularly Fire Under the Snow, without which I imagine the
publication in Canada of this important book
would have been very different."
~Katharina Bielenberg, export manager, Harvill Books

"I am disheartened to hear that you will be leaving.
You have been wonderful and a pleasure to work with."
~Eric Price, export manager, GroveAtlantic Press

"I'm aghast! What will we do without you? It has
been a pleasure working with you."
~Sara Davis, publicity director, Globe-Pequot Press

"All has gone well, according to some well laid plans. So the time has
come to properly acknowledge your enthusiastic and able assistance. On
behalf of James and the rest of us at The Urban Peasant,
thank-you, thank-you, thank-you."
~Romey Grant, producer, The Urban Peasant

"We should add Salman to this, he has classy ideas =)"
~Leandro Rodrigues, head creative at TEGG Brazil

"Have you ever had an unknown, uninvited guest who turned out to be
God's gift in person? Meet Salman. Originally, he was just meant to spend
a few days on his way in and out of Afghanistan. If ever you're looking for
the perfect definition of "Hausfreund" (even the monolingual English
speakers will figure this one out I trust), Salman couldn't be beat. Ah, the
delicious food he cooks. Ah, the way he's always there to help when you
need him, yet never in the way. Ah, how he inspires, nurtures and deepens
conversations. Btw, he's still traveling, so if you like, I can share his email.
We ended up going to the Pamirs with Surat (Tajik friend whom I've been
trying to help strengthen his tour agency: www.pamir-adventure.com)

and an awesome Aussie by the name of Nathan who'd decided on a whim to travel home via Central Asia (has he started his Café d'Orient yet?)."
~Munira Chudoba, Bishkek, Kyrgyzstan

AUTHORS/CREATORS

"From one believer in the magic to another."
~Terry Brooks, author of The Sword of Shannara (Del Rey)

"For Sal: 'You wade through shit and then you find a Johna?'
—W.S. Burroughs. Many Many thanks for everything."
~Will Self author of Great Apes (Grove Atlantic)

"To Sal who tried a lot harder than some to sell this. Thanks mate."
~Nick Bantock author of the Griffin and Sabine trilogy (Chronicle Books)

"Thanks for single handedly quadrupling my vast Thornhill sales!
Much appreciated."
~Garfield Reeves-Stevens, author of Children of the Shroud (Doubleday)

"To Sal, my agent, my hero and my friend."
~Patrick Taylor, author of Pray for Us Sinners (Insomniac Press)

"Your super organization left very little for me to cover.
Thanks again for the great tour. Let's do it again."
~James McNair, cookbook author (Chronicle)

"Sal, thank you for your company."
~John de Lance, actor, Q on Star Trek: The Next Generation

"Bolshoi Splasiba for his friend."
~Martin Cruz Smith author of Gorky Park (Random House)

"Thanks for the guided tour of Toronto."
~Peter Arnett, CNN correspondent and author of Live from the Battlefield
(Simon & Schuster)

"You are one of the best pitch-men I know."
~Mark Russell, Editor, writer and other word stuff

"I have published several books with Sal, and he's definitely someone you want on your side through good and bad. You hear this sort of thing a lot, but Sal's communications skills really are incredible. Whether dealing with editors and printers, or running authors through the media circus, you can rely on him to know who's doing what, where the problems are, and how to fix them. The man networks better than anyone I've seen."
~William Hopper, Author at ERIS

"With my thanks for connecting me with this exceptional experience!"
~Marion Raycheba co-author of *The Living Workplace* (HarperCollins)

"Thank you so much for all your hard work. Your attention to all the details was very much appreciated by Roy and myself. Thanks again."
~Wendy, assistant to Roy Henry Vickers, artist (Raincoast)

"Many thanks for a delightful media day in Toronto.
You're an excellent host."
~Jennifer Darling, editor of *The New Cookbook*
(Better Homes and Gardens)

"For Sal, who made it happen!"
~Terence M. Green, foreword to *Sunburst* by Phyllis Gotlieb (Bakka Books)

"I highly recommend Salman and thoroughly enjoyed working with him on publicizing my second CD release. He had inventive promotion concepts, and even went above and beyond to assist and oversee with booking the jazz festival circuit. You'd have to look far and wide to find this kind of care and commitment.I would work
with him again, anytime."
~Vincent Wolfe, Recording Artist & CEO, GEM Prod./V-Jazz Records

"Sal is that rarest of things: a publisher brimming with creativity and passion, who understands real-world marketing and satisfying the consumer, and how those mesh with and enhance published products."
~Ed Greenwood, Freelance Writing and Game Design

"Sal has the unparalleled ability to see the big picture, cut through the extraneous garbage, and help you look like a winner."
~Mark Russell, Editor, writer and other word stuff

"Should everything go horribly wrong and everything screw up, he's going to be able to patch together a solution nobody knew was possible. Lastly, no review of Sal's abilities would be complete without mentioning that he is always able to find the best food and the best restaurants in any city. It is a gift that those around him rely on for the perfect business meetings."
~William Hopper, Author at ERIS

"Indefatigable."
~Elaine Cunningham, author

"The one constant I could come to depend on."
~Corbin Salmon, author

"Most of all, a hearty CONGRATULATIONS
and heartfelt THANK YOU."
~Barbara Letson, author

"Thank you for all You have done."
~Richard Harris, author

"Much appreciated...May the wind have your back."
~Martin Treanor, author of Fall of Ancients (Fire Hornet Codex)

"Thanks for maintaining your faith in me for so long."
~John Crispo author of Rebel Without a Pause (Warwick)

"Whatever the project you're working on, Sal has the unparalleled ability to see the big picture, cut through the extraneous garbage, and help you look like a winner. He's intolerant of mediocrity and is definitely someone you want to work with if your goal is excellence."
~Mark Russell, Editor, writer and other word stuff

"Congratulations on promoting the impossible. Many thanks."
~John Crispo, professor of management at the University of Toronto and author of *Making Canada Work* (Random House)

"With gratitude for the wonderful work you are doing on our behalf, and for making our Toronto experience so enjoyable."
~Terrance and Pamela Sweeny, authors of *What God Hath Joined* (Random House)

"What would we have done without you? ... Toronto tour
was perfect and we will always be grateful."
~Terrance and Pamela Sweeny, authors of *What God Hath Joined*
(Random House)

"This letter is to commend the outstanding service provided to us by Sal
Nensi. ... There's a commercial motto which says, 'You're in good hands
with Allstate.' Pamela and I feel Allstate could
learn a few things from Sal!"
~Terrance and Pamela Sweeny, authors of *What God Hath Joined*
(Random House)

"Thanks so much. Here's to travelling around the
country doing crazy book things."
~Todd Babiak author of Choke Hold (Turnstone Press)

"Many thanks for your friendship and your hard work."
~Garfield Reeves-Stevens, author of *Night Eyes* (Foundation)

"Much love to you Sal!"
~Josephine Cox, author of *Cradle of Thorns* (Headline Books)

"For Lovely Sal whose smile welcomed me to Toronto!
Have a magic, charmed life."
~Titania Hardie, author of *Enchanted* (Quadrille)

"Thanks for being our guide and our dinner companion."
~Mason Wiley and Damien Bona, authors of *Inside Oscar* (Random House)

"Thanks for all the great work."
~Scott Mowbray, author of *The Food Fight* (Random House)

"Best wishes and appreciation for all your efforts!"
~Samuel Osherson, author of *Wrestling with Love* (Fawcett)

"Thanks for the great publicity job."
~Betty Zyvatkauskas, author of *Great Getaways*
(Random House of Canada)

"Thank you for making my book a success."
~Dr. Earl Mindel, author of *Food as Medicine* (Fireside)

"I felt the book signings, interviews, etc... went well! Had a lot of fun!
My thanks for a job "well done"!"
~Diane Clement, cookbook author (Raincoast)

"With great thanks for introducing us to the world of
publicity with such comfort and style."
~Lauren Cowen, author of *Daughters and Mothers* (Courage Books)

"Thanks for all the help."
~Jack Nisbet, author of *Sources of the River* (Sasquatch Books)

"Sal was such a pleasure."
~Erica Ehm, editor (*What's Up Kids* magazine)

"You're amazing because you're kind and funny and generous and you
have a remarkable brain. I don't know anyone else who thinks like you."
~Sandra Kasturi, editor and writer

"That was a fun website."
~Mark Russell, Editor, writer and other word stuff

"This book would never be without you—so you
really do have my eternal gratitude!"
~Sandra Kasturi editor of *The Stars as Seen* (Red Deer Press)

"You are a lovely, funny, wonderful man, with a
brain that works like no one else's."
~Brett Savory, editor and writer

STORYTELLING, WRITING & CREATIVITY

"You do dialogue-bounce to scene-setting authorial voice
bounce right back to dialogue really well…"
~Ed Greenwood, president, The Ed Greenwood Group

"'Creativity' takes on a whole new meaning when I'm riffing with you. It's
not just that you make it feel like anything is possible, but also that you
have an eye on the COMPLETE cycle . . . as in "what happens AFTER we
make it." THAT'S a rare treat for me and makes the "dreaming" quality of
riffing less intangible. We want to change the world and dreams
are only the START of that noble cause."
~Dave Robison, vice president The Ed Greenwood Group

"The fact that "Stealing a Rickshaw" is not a posthumous story about Sal,
clearly shows that he is a man who 'really knows where his towel is'."
~Dileep Rangan, illustrator (Singapore)

"You are crazy. That is totally fine."
~Alex Kammer, GameHole Con

"You've got great shit going on in your head …
it's fucking brilliant, I love it."
~Martin Treanor, creative partner

"Enjoyed the interview. Thanks."
~Nick Bantock, author of the Griffin and Sabine Trilogy
(Chronicle Books)

"It seems a new kind of experience for me, like, I was travelling every
corner of the world with your travel experience. I was impressed about
the attitude of saying no towards the Alcohol Sachet business and a lot
more concerned about ecological. I really appreciate that. I'm eagerly
waiting to get this one published in the book
and wishing it to get success."
~Krishna Moothy, Transcriber, *How To Steal a Rickshaw* (Zariqa.com)

"Ask Salman a question and he'll take you on a journey across many lands, diverse cultures, and brain-popping experiences. To hear one of his adventures is an adventure in itself. I could, and have done on many occasions, listened to him for hours . . . becoming all the wiser for it."
~Martin Treanor, author and illustrator: *The Silver Mist*, The Tales of Trumplethinskin trilogy, and forthcoming Fall of Ancients trilogy

"*Too Late Now . . . Pass The Kebabs!*" is filled with humour, joie de vivre, and unvarnished unbiased observations of the features of our world —both good and bad."
~Steve Bowden, author *Awaken The Used Car Salesman Within* (Fire Hornet Codex)

"Let me tell you a story . . ." and with those words, you lean in and prepare yourself to hear something wonderful or weird or shocking. It's human nature . . . you can't help it. But when Salman Nensi says it, trust me . . . you AREN'T prepared for what's to come. Salman has walked the rarefied halls of the corporate elite and the back alleys of Bhutan. He's eaten, smoked, and savored things that are only hinted at in most people's experience, and he's walked, rickshawed, flown, and ran through streets that most people didn't know existed. So when Sal says he wants to tell you a story, you better buckle up . . . because he's taking you on an e-ticket ride to a world you've never seen before."
~Dave Robison, ButteryManVoice.com

"Very engaging writing style, Sal—just like when you tell stories verbally. This is your strongest suit. . . . McDermid was right—you're a good writer, and I agree that you could sell this shit to a big house with all the stories you have. No doubt of it."
~Brett Savory, author (Hobb's Editions)

"I really enjoyed this too! You have a real knack for showing the flavour of the place. Some of it reminds me of some of Henry Rollins's travel stories (which are really funny). You could be the Gay Bill Bryson!"
~Sandra Kasturi, author (Muttonchop Editions)

CONTACT

Voicemail only: +1 905.882.4696

Email: salmannensi@gmail.com

Residences: Toronto | London

Citizenship: dual British & Canadian

NENSI.COM

www.ingramcontent.com/pod-product-compliance
Lightning Source LLC
Chambersburg PA
CBHW040244230326
41458CB00104B/6474